Children
of Separation
and Loss

A Memoir

Gertrude Pollitt

Hamilton Books

A member of
Rowman & Littlefield
Lanham • Boulder • New York • Toronto • Plymouth, UK

X

Copyright © 2014 by Hamilton Books
4501 Forbes Boulevard, Suite 200, Lanham, Maryland 20706
Hamilton Books Aquisitions Department (301) 459-3366

10 Thornbury Road, Plymouth PL6 7PP, United Kingdom

Library of Congress Control Number: 2014932489
ISBN: 978-0-7618-6341-0 (paper : alk. paper)—ISBN: 978-0-7618-6342-7 (electronic)

Cover photo: One of the kibbutz groups from Poland, Camp Aschau. The banner says "Going forward to the Hebrew State to freedom."

♾™ The paper used in this publication meets the minimum requirements of American National Standard for Information Sciences Permanence of Paper for Printed Library Materials, ANSI/NISO Z39.48-1992.

To my late cousins Arnold and Ruth Stein and their sons
Michael, Joel, and David for their tireless determination
and relentless efforts to search for me over a period of eight years.

Contents

Acknowledgments

I wish to thank Robin Lira for encouraging me to write the book in the first place, and Nancy Rosenfeld and Liz Peterson for their unflagging enthusiasm and tireless efforts on my behalf.

I take full responsibility for the opinions expressed in this book, as well as for any errors or inaccuracies. I would also like to thank my clients and/or patients who gave me permission to use their case material in this book. In each instance their name and circumstances have been altered to preserve confidentiality.

Prologue

On the morning of March 17, 1939, I was making my bed and straightening my room when the radio announced that the Nazis had invaded Czechoslovakia, the model democratic state in Europe. As soon as my mother returned from grocery shopping, I told her the news. She turned pale. "Darling, you'll have to leave," she said. "Now."

"Now? Alone?" I asked. "Can't you come with me?"

We had discussed this many times before, and I knew what her answer would be. She always pointed out that she was old, not well enough to travel, that Uncle Filip and Aunt Paula would take care of her, that they'd been good citizens, that the Germans didn't know they were Jewish and would not harm them. After going through the entire litany again, she headed toward my room to help me pack.

I realized then that my family would never leave Vienna voluntarily. They had convinced themselves that nothing would happen to them, a massive denial on their part. How could Vienna be safe for them but not for me? If the Nazis found out they were Jewish, they would either be shot on the spot or beaten and sent to a concentration camp. We had seen that happening all around us every day since the Anschluss a year before. My papers were in order and I knew that I had to leave, but when my family refused to go with me, I felt rejected.

We packed clothes, toilet articles, and family photographs into the large brown leather suitcase which had belonged to my father and had not been used since his death seven years before. Mother called her travel agent who recommended a train that left late that evening and traveled through Germany to Hoek van Holland, a port town in the Netherlands where I could catch a ferry to England. Mother hired a taxi and we spent the afternoon traveling all over the city in search of English currency. The banks either had none or didn't want to part with what they had. By the end of the day we had accumulated a grand total of one pound and fifteen shillings. Uncle Filip suggested that I take some jewelry with me inside the back of a hairbrush, but I was afraid. If anyone discovered I was smuggling jewelry, it could cost me my life.

Mother, Aunt Paula, and Uncle Filip accompanied me to the railroad station. I was still angry and hurt that they had refused to come with me. As we stood on the platform waiting for the train, we couldn't pretend that this was a normal occasion, and no one could find much to say. Mother said she was sorry, in all the commotion she had forgotten to pack me a lunch. Aunt Paula asked me to be sure to write the moment I touched English soil, to let them know I was safe. As the train pulled in, they all hugged and kissed me goodbye. Uncle Filip hoisted my suitcase onto the train, gave me an extra hug, and told me, "You'll be fine." I found a seat by a window and took a long last look at them in an attempt to memorize their faces. The faces blurred and I felt tears on my cheeks before it struck me that I might never see any of them again.

The train was not crowded at first, but soon it began to fill up with refugees, most of them men, most of them probably Jewish, who were loaded down with suitcases and bundles, as if trying to take all their possessions with them. Some men carried duffel bags and looked to me like deserters from the German army. As the train wound its way through Germany, the lights were off but no one slept. Grown men were biting their fingernails and when the conductor walked through to punch tickets, people stiffened and looked at the floor. There was free-floating anxiety everywhere because everyone feared being discovered and sent back.

I huddled against the window and tried not to think. As I gazed out the window into the night, my childhood with all its joys and sorrows passed before me. What my future would be I could not imagine. From time to time I put my hand in my pocket to reassure myself that everything was there—the English currency, my English labor permit which had arrived a few weeks before from an unknown source, and my Czech passport, a legacy from my father which permitted me to travel almost anywhere without a visa and was not imprinted with "J" or "Jude."

The train stopped at the Dutch border the following day. Dutch border guards in gray-green uniforms climbed onto the train and began to stamp everyone's passports. The Dutch were known to hate the Nazis, and at first it looked as if everyone would be allowed to pass through to safety. I permitted myself to breathe.

A border guard approached the elderly woman in the seat across the aisle from me. He looked at her passport but did not return it, a Czech passport, I noticed, just like mine. I handed him my passport. He kept that also, and taking both passports with him, left the train. The woman and I glanced at each other wondering what it could mean.

We did not have long to wonder. A megaphone blasted out our names, and a loud and penetrating voice told us "Aussteigen!" Both of us got off the train. The whistle blew in preparation for departure. As the train pulled away huffing and puffing, someone tossed our bags through an open window onto the platform.

A border guard approached and informed us, "Your passports are worthless. Czechoslovakia no longer exists. You'll have to return to your homes." He handed the passports back to us.

It was hard to believe—to have made it all the way through Germany unmolested to be stopped just a stone's throw from freedom. I was stunned. But nothing could make me return to streets swarming with Nazi sadists. Mustering all my courage, I told the guard that I had to be in London to tend to a very sick aunt. When he looked skeptical, I became more eloquent and a little hysterical. With a shrug of his shoulders, he pronounced that I could go on, but the elderly woman would have to go back to Czechoslovakia, now occupied by Nazis. Her wrinkled face turned white and my heart went out to her. I wished I could take her with me.

I was standing on the platform at a loss to know what to do next when a well-dressed middle-aged man with a well-groomed beard approached me. He recognized my distress and spoke to me calmly, explaining that he was from the Joint Distribution Committee whose purpose was to help desolate Jews wherever they happened to find themselves.

I felt I could trust this man, and I told him everything.

He assured me that my passport was valid. "Border guards these days are all a little crazy," he said. "They probably think you're a spy. God knows you don't look like a refugee. You're too well dressed."

My benefactor—I never found out his name—bought me a ticket for the next train to Hoek van Holland. I offered him my English currency, which he courteously refused, and before I could express my gratitude, he pressed the ticket into my hand and disappeared into the dark shadows of the station.

Chapter One

Childhood in Vienna

I was born in Vienna in 1919, just after the end of the First World War, to a *haut bourgeois* family. There was no Marshall plan, and war-torn Austria was not only defeated but depleted.

I was a healthy, hefty baby, weighing eight pounds at birth, but there was a problem—how and where to obtain milk. My mother was unable to breast-feed me for medical reasons. Austrians were starving, and milk was not available in Vienna.[1] She might have hired a wet nurse from the Tyrol where there were wet nurses in abundance. Thanks to a custom known as "win-dowling," which involved a young man climbing through his girlfriend's bedroom window and spending the night with her, many babies were born out of wedlock. They were welcomed in the country, since the farmers always needed more hands to help with the work. This tolerant point of view was not common in Vienna, where Victorian morality was the rule, and Mother preferred not to have "one of those girls" in our house. Fortunately for me, Father was able to come up with a solution.

Father was a native of Bohemia, part of the newly created Czechoslova-kia, where farm products were still available. Like his father before him, he was a wholesale merchant of rawhides and skins. He began to make regular trips by train to Bohemia where he still had friends and was able to trade balls of fur for cans of milk. He smuggled the milk over the border by wrapping the milk cans in fur. On one of his return trips the border guard questioned him as to the contents of the fur balls. Before Father could come up with an answer, the guard stuck his bayonet into one of the fur balls and milk spurted out in a big stream. The guard was not above taking a bribe, and all Father had to do to be allowed to pass through was to give him a can of milk. In our pantry at home we had drawers full of sugar and flour that Father had procured in Bohemia. My parents distributed these staples to our relatives and friends to help them stave off starvation.

FIRST MEMORIES

There is a story told so often in our family that I seem to remember it, even though I was barely two when it happened. One day on a trip to the park, I swallowed a stone. Back home I looked up at Mother and said the German equivalent of "Me swallow stoney." Mother put both hands to her face and opened her mouth wide but didn't utter a sound. This had me worried, so I revised my story and said, "Me *not* swallow stoney." Mother was confused. Had I or had I not swallowed a stone? I kept her in suspense by pointing to my stomach from time to time and declaring "Here is stoney!" only to deny it the next minute. Mother purchased a small glass chamber pot in order to observe my bowel movements. I finally declared that the stone was coming and eliminated a rather large, oval, well-polished stone, much to everyone's relief. Mother kept the stone in a jewel box in her dresser and showed it off to guests on special occasions.

When I was three and a half, my parents took me to see my first play, "Little Red Riding Hood." I followed the story closely. As the climax approached, Red Riding Hood said, "Grandma, what big teeth you have!" to which the wolf replied, "The better to eat you with, my dear!" Before the wolf had time to jump out of bed and swallow Red Riding Hood whole, I rose to my feet and called down from our box in my loudest voice, "Mr. Wolf, please do *not* eat Red Riding Hood!" It stopped the show.

When I was four, Mother enrolled me in a rhythmical dance group which met in people's homes and was taught by a qualified dance instructor. I clearly remember our first performance. In a costume of green crepe paper, with two little lights on my head, I danced the part of the glow worm to Paul Linke's "Das Glühwürmchen," whose words in English are "Shine, little glow worm, glimmer, glimmer…." My entire family was there to watch and applaud as I threw myself into the part and became the glow worm, at least for the duration of the song.

FAMILY

My father, Julius Stein, grew up in Bohemia in a village so small that it had to be identified by naming two nearby towns plus the river along which the village lay. Thus he came from *Novy Oetting, Vzelnice, Kamenice, na Lipau.* He was the oldest of five children. I do not know my father's educational background, but he was well versed in art, music, and literature and was proficient in German, Czech, and Hebrew. His friends used to call him "Herr

Professor." These days he would be called a Renaissance Man. He was a romantic, and when away on business trips, he would write to my mother exclusively in verse. This was Father's second marriage. After the death of his first wife, he and his daughter Martha, in her early teens, had moved to Vienna where he met and married my mother. Father was a devout Jew, more conservative than Mother. He said his prayers and he laid his tefillin every morning. Friday evenings were always celebrated with the lighting of candles and a bracha prayer spoken over my head. We belonged to a Conservative temple and celebrated all Jewish holidays, with Father presiding.

Father had a Czech passport, which he valued greatly because he identified with his primary family, his upbringing, and Czechoslovakia, a democratic country which was thriving economically, socially, and culturally. On several occasions Father was asked to take on Austrian nationality, which he chose not to do. As a result, our family was considered foreigners and he had to pay more in certain taxes. When I was enrolled in a private high school, he had to pay double tuition. That my father held fast to his decision meant that I too had a Czech passport, which ultimately saved my life.

My mother, Sidonie Brauch, had an older sister, Paula, and a younger brother, Filip. They had emigrated to Vienna with their parents from Transylvania, which kept changing hands between Hungary and Rumania. The town they came from was called *Lugos* in Hungarian and *Lugoi* in Rumania. For high school my mother attended an excellent Catholic school in a convent and was fluent in Hungarian, Rumanian, and German. She shared my father's interest in music, literature, and art.

Mother was forty-five when I was born and Father was sixty. Because of the advanced age of both of my parents, my family began to shrink when I was young and I didn't have many relatives. When I was born, my maternal grandmother was the only one of my grandparents still alive. Mother had cousins in Hungary and Vienna whom we saw occasionally. Father's sister Aida, who lived in the United States, came to visit from time to time, as did his sister Olga, a well known actress in Berlin. Otto, the youngest of Father's siblings, married a Polish girl, lived in New York, had three sons, and was in the insurance business. When he arrived in New York, he changed his name to Arthur and Father never heard from him again.

Both my parents were tall and stately, towering over people of average height. Father sported a mustache and a small, well-trimmed beard, which was the fashion in those days. He was stout but held himself very erect. At that time Europeans considered stoutness not a health hazard but a sign of wealth. Especially amongst the lower classes, being overweight meant that one had enough money to indulge oneself with food. Mother, who was not overweight, was beautiful by any standard, with a small nose, a small mouth, and a rosy complexion. She had a regal appearance, partly because, like

Father, she held herself erect. In her younger years, she wore her hair on the top of her head in a twisted bun.

EARLY YEARS

My early years were good ones. Father's daughter Martha, who was fifteen years my senior, was more like an aunt than a sister, so I was raised as an only child, doted on and indulged. It was easy to win the admiration of my family. All I had to do was the things most babies do and they acted as if a miracle had occurred. As an infant, I moved all my fingers in a rhythmical way and stared at them intently. From this, my family concluded that I was bright. My hair was straight, plentiful, strawberry blond, and neatly parted on one side, which made me look like a boy. This didn't bother them in the least. They put a bow in my hair and predicted that I would soon be as tall and beautiful as Mother. I guess I was a little spoiled. It seemed to me that the household revolved around me, and perhaps for a while it did.

Father liked to read to me and tell me bedtime stories. He was very creative and made up stories with cowboys and Indians in them. Some of his stories began with the plot of a play or an opera he'd seen and went on from there. He frequently drew his inspiration from the lyrics of arias, his favorites being those accompanied by flute. When I was past the toddler stage, Father took me for frequent strolls around the Ringstrasse, the street surrounding the center of Vienna with its government buildings and churches and opera house, and implanted in me his love of nature, something he had acquired in the village where he grew up. He would admire the lilacs and chestnut trees and examine every bush and flower, calling them by their Latin names and making me very much aware of the beauty of growing plants. On Sunday afternoons Father and I and sometimes Martha would go to the Prater, an amusement park for children and the young at heart. Here I enjoyed the carousel, the haunted house, and riding the tired-out horses. Best of all was the Ferris wheel, a landmark for the Viennese. The cars, shaped like the cars of a train, could accommodate about ten people each. As we dangled from the superstructure, we could see all of Vienna and the countryside beyond.

Mother did not accompany us on these outings. As a child, she had suffered from rheumatic heart disease which left her with an enlarged heart. She couldn't walk far or go up the slightest incline without experiencing breathlessness and palpitations of the heart. In spite of this, she was an excellent manager and took charge of my upbringing and education. She recorded my progress in a baby book—first tooth, weaning from the bottle, toilet training, first words, first sentences. Mother enrolled me in a private nursery school and managed my social life, arranging times for me to play with other children. To keep me from becoming too spoiled, she gave me a few simple jobs to do, such as putting my toys away when I was through playing with them. She was an excellent Hungarian-style cook and from an early age I helped her out in the kitchen. This was a task I enjoyed, especially when she made a torte and allowed me to sample the many delicious cream fillings.

I can't remember who gave me my favorite toys—probably Mother—but I do remember vividly what they were. There was a large blond teddy bear with whom I slept. When I moved his tail, he could either nod his head "yes" or shake his head "no." I frequently used the bear to express my feelings, and it was Teddy who said *yes* or *no* on my behalf. Another favorite toy was a gorgeous Käte Kruse doll the size of an infant, with a hand-painted face, rosy cheeks, real brown hair and eyelashes, and deep blue eyes that opened and closed. When I picked her up, she would open her mouth and say "Mummy." This doll wore my baby clothes and when taken for a ride in a buggy, was often mistaken for a real baby girl. Two other toys I cherished were a doll-house-sized bathroom with working fixtures and a golliwog, a rag doll with red hair and rosy cheeks.

Martha, who was enrolled in Gustav Klimt's School of Arts and Crafts, instilled in me a life-long interest in art. I loved to watch her as she painted features on the silk faces of the dolls she had made. These were not small dolls for children to play with but large adult dolls to be treated with respect and used for home decoration. We had several of them gracing couches and easy chairs all over the house. Martha and I were good friends. She drew flowers and animals and people for me, made sure that I always had plenty of art supplies, and encouraged me in my early artistic endeavors. Martha was not only a talented artist but an accomplished pianist as well. Our family never grew tired of hearing her play Beethoven's "Moonlight Sonata." It made a pleasant background for our activities as it echoed around the house.

Uncle Filip, Aunt Paula, and Grandmother lived together in a flat not far from ours, and we saw all three of them several times a week. Uncle Filip, a jeweler, managed a store in Marienbad, a well known European spa in Czechoslovakia, and supported Grandmother and Aunt Paula. He was tall, slim, and handsome, with a picturesque hairstyle, cut short. He was a sharp dresser and wore well-tailored, British-style suits. His friends called him "The Englishman." He loved classical music and played the violin, often with small chamber groups, for a musical evening at our house. I was expected to sit quietly and listen, like a well-bred adult. Although Uncle Filip had a girlfriend, he never married. He was devoted to us, his primary family, and thought of me as the child he never had.

Aunt Paula seemed to think of me that way also. Like Martha, she played the piano but only one piece—Beethoven's "Für Elise"—which became a little tedious after a while. One day I asked her if she ever played anything else. She said she used to play all sorts of pieces but that was years ago and she didn't have time to work them up again. I could see why. An expert in fancy needlework, she spent several hours each day sewing, tatting, embroidering, doing needlepoint and petit point, and making lace. Long before I reached adolescence, she started making napkins, tablecloths, pillowcases, curtains, and bedspreads for my dowry. Aunt Paula told me that she had once been engaged to be married but the plans fell through. She never told me the details and I never asked.

Grandmother was healthy when I was small and enjoyed telling me stories of her childhood, but as I grew older, she started to fade away. Not long before she died, at age seventy-seven, she heard a famous opera singer on the radio and said to Mother, "That man has a lovely voice. Why don't you offer him a cup of tea."

The two helpers in our house were almost like members of the family. There was Vettie, a middle-aged Czech woman who lived with us, shared the cooking and housekeeping tasks with Mother, and acted as my nanny. Vettie took great care of me and I loved her dearly. The other helper was my governess, a Viennese girl called Lisa. She took me on outings to various parks including Schönbrunn, the palace of Kaiser Franz Joseph, whose extensive French-style gardens had beautiful flowerbeds. Lisa also took me to her church where she prayed faithfully nearly every day. When she encouraged me to kneel and make the sign of the cross, I gladly complied. I was impressed with the pomp and splendor of the church and with everything it represented. Needless to say, I did not tell my parents. Even at this early age I sensed that Father especially would take a dim view of my embracing the Catholic religion.

ZU DER SONNE

My family lived at 37 Neubaugasse in the Seventh District in an Art Deco style building called *Zu der Sonne*, meaning "To the Sun." The wrought iron entrance gate had a wrought iron sun at the top. There was a life-sized centaur in bas relief on the wall in the front hall. The winding stairwell, paved with marble, had three large stained glass windows depicting baskets overflowing with flowers. Our flat, one of six in the building, was elegant and spacious. We had Persian carpets covering parquet floors, and almost all of our furniture was custom made, some in the Biedermeier style and some in Art Deco. One of the leather couches was covered with a Persian carpet, like the famous analytic couch of Sigmund Freud. A Bösendorfer grand piano and an elaborate crystal chandelier graced our dining room. Both of my parents were collectors of beautiful things. Mother collected various *objets d'art* such as porcelain figurines, antique silver, demitasses from all over Europe, and bowls, trays, and wine glasses made of cut crystal. Father had a large collection of original paintings that he purchased at exhibitions. Father's and my favorite was hung on the dining room wall where we could enjoy it every day—an Albrecht Dürer etching entitled *The Young Boy.*

Each room in our house contained a large, decorative, glazed-tile oven whose color matched the décor of the room, wine-red for the dining room, green for the living room, and yellow for my room. In winter the heat of the ovens radiated an even temperature throughout the house. Our beds were made up with a deerskin under the sheets and a huge eiderdown comforter to keep us warm.

My parents' room was stunning. Mother's dressing table, in the Art Deco style, had three mirrors. All the furniture was made of reddish burled chestnut set against lilac wallpaper. Of course, the oven in their room was lilac to match the walls. My room was adjacent to my parents' room. To get from my room to theirs, I had to walk through a secret door, across about three feet of parquet floor, through another secret door. The secret doors were scarcely visible because, unlike the big double doors in the rest of the house, they were covered with the same wallpaper as the walls. As a young child, I loved to climb into my parents' bed to be reassured or to hear one of Father's stories. Before I fell asleep, my parents would send me back to my own bed, something I resisted but learned to tolerate. After graduating from my crib, I landed in a brass bed with blue trimmings and my very own eiderdown. The rest of the room was in yellow with blue touches. To this day, yellow and blue are the predominant colors I use for decorating my place.

It took a great deal of work to keep our house in order. In summer the carpets were cleaned, rolled up, stuffed with mothballs, and put away. So were the velvet curtains, which were removed from the large windows, leaving only the white gauze curtains with tatted inlays and making the entire flat feel airy and light. In winter the tile ovens, which used bricks of slow-burning coal, had to be cleaned out every day. Then there were all the routine tasks such as cooking, washing, ironing, and polishing silver and wood and floors. Vettie did most of this, but it was too much for one person. Mother and Martha helped out, and when I was old enough, so did I.

A CLOUD IN MY SKY

I was four years old when I first realized that my life was not perfect. Mother spent a lot of time with Martha to help her become adjusted to her new family and deal with feelings concerning the loss of her mother, which were intensified when Father married Mother. Too young to understand this, I was jealous. During some holiday seasons Mother would go off with Martha to a fashionable vacation spot and be gone for several days. They left me at home with Vettie, and I resented it. When they finally returned, I would ignore them and cling to Vettie, to show them just how much I didn't care.

I found another good way to rebel. Whenever someone at the dinner table complained about the food, I would rise from the table, walk into the kitchen, and tell Vettie that they were talking behind her back. This, I hoped, made it clear to everyone that my first loyalty lay with Vettie. Although I repeated this type of behavior on several occasions, my parents understood that expressions of anger and hostility were part of growing up and did not punish me. They labeled me *l'enfant terrible* and let it go at that.

TRAVEL

During the summer my family sometimes traveled for two or three months at a time. I was included on these vacations. Vettie and Lisa came along to help take care of me. Sometimes Uncle Filip, Aunt Paula, and Grandmother came with us, and Father would join us for weekends, when he could get away from his work.

We usually stayed in Austria's lake district at fashionable resorts such as Ischl, Gmunden, and Attersee (the town) on Attersee (the lake). Sometimes Father's sister Aida from the United States would join us. Aunt Aida, like Father, was tall and stout. She had a large protruding bosom, which to me meant motherliness, and, indeed, her behavior towards me was quite maternal. While vacationing in Austria, the women in our family often wore *dirndls*, the Austrian national costume which originated with peasants in the Alps. The costume consisted of a long, full skirt, a puffy blouse, a tight-fitting vest, an apron, and sometimes a large triangular scarf thrown over the shoulders. Father did not wear lederhosen, the leather shorts often worn by Austrian men and boys, because he considered himself not Austrian but Czech.

During the summer months my grandmother and Aunt Paula usually rented an apartment in Baden bei Wien, a resort mainly for the elderly, and sometimes Mother and I would join them there. A band called the "Kurkapelle" played in the sizable, well-landscaped park. A special feature of the resort was a theater with a sliding glass roof that could be closed in inclement weather. Here we attended Franz Lehar operettas and concerts given by famous singers including the famous Austrian tenor, Richard Tauber.

Sometimes we ventured beyond Austria to German towns by the North Sea. Judging from some old photographs that I occasionally revisit, the air was often too cold for swimming. Several photos show us sitting on the beach fully dressed. In some pictures I appear to be camera shy. All you can see of me is the large bow in my hair and my head bent down towards a book. In most pictures, though, I am not shy at all and face the camera head on.

We spent some of our vacations in Czechoslovakia, often with family and friends, always with Father visiting for a few days. On one occasion he asked the band to play a particular waltz that both my parents liked. He and Mother, the only pair on the dance floor, danced this waltz with passion. Seeing my parents like this made me feel happy and secure.

The other foreign country we visited was Switzerland. I remember that in Lucerne Martha had several young men vying for her attention. They made use of me to find out all sorts of things about her, information I happily supplied.

MARTHA

When Martha was twenty, she was determined to get married. All her girl-friends were getting married and she felt she should too. She found a man, a Czech who claimed to be a university-degreed engineer, to whom she became engaged. This was fine with me because Egon, the groom-to-be, paid attention me. We had a big engagement party at which everyone behaved in a way that struck me as strange. Mother had bought a costly new set of china which was ceremoniously broken into pieces. Every guest at the party received a broken piece with a ribbon tied around it. I thought this custom to be highly uncivilized. No one bothered to tell me what it signified. If it was meant to keep an engagement from being broken, it did its work too well.

Father made Egon a partner in his business. I was aware that a large sum of money had been put aside for Martha's dowry, and I knew that Mother gave Martha valuable jewelry, including an umbrella broach made of Burmese rubies, which I cherished. Despite the elaborate preparations, Martha was not happy. Both my parents encouraged her to break off the engagement, but she refused.

For me, the wedding was a great occasion, celebrated with dignity, splendor, and pomp. I was a six-year-old bridesmaid and wore a spectacular dress made of pink pleated silk trimmed with ecru handmade lace. On my left shoulder there was a bouquet of pink roses perched on a blue velvet bow whose streamers reached down to my knees and waved in the wind while I had an unsupervised ball and got sick from eating too much ice cream.

Six months later Martha was found dead on her kitchen floor, poisoned by gas fumes. My parents told everyone it was an accident, but I sensed they were not telling the whole story and I pieced things together bit by bit. Martha had told my parents that she was miserable. One reason for this was that Egon was pathologically frugal and continuously threatened her that if they didn't hold on to their money, they would soon be begging on the streets. They started off for a honeymoon in Italy but got off the train at Semmering in Austria because it would cost less money. Martha was used to affluence and was frustrated and angry when her husband withheld money that had been given to both of them by her father. Mother and Father suggested an annulment, but Martha ignored their advice.

Martha's suicide was a great shock to all of us. Father took her death especially hard. Never before had I seen my father cry. Though I was only six years old, he insisted that I attend the funeral. Many friends were shocked to see me there, but I think that Father was right to include me. It gave me some sense of closure to this traumatic event. The loss of my sister, compounded by my father's profound grief, had a deep and lasting effect on me. Adding salt to an open wound, Martha's husband, the con man, did not show up at the funeral, absconded with the dowry, and was never heard from again.

Martha's death was the first of three traumas I suffered when I was six. The second was when Lisa resigned to get married. I was still mourning the loss of Martha, and for me, this second loss was overwhelming. Even though Lisa did not live with us and never discussed what went on in her private life, I had felt she was a member of our family. Perhaps she chose this time frame because I, at six, was about to start grammar school and would not need her so much any more. More probably she was not astute enough to realize how devastating Martha's death had been for me. Lisa and I parted as friends. I had sensed in advance that she was going to leave, since she had started to withdraw from me emotionally.

The third traumatic event for me at age six was starting grammar school. To me, this was one more loss, as if my carefree childhood had come to an end. It was also a great steppingstone, and I felt anxious and insecure. I would have to get to school on time, follow a regular schedule, and do homework and all the rest that is required of a first grader. I spent the first day of school sick at home in bed. Mother stood by me and helped me feel strong enough to attend school the following day.

The school was a public grammar school within easy walking distance of my home. It included grades one through four, with only one teacher for all four grades. The classes were large, with about forty students per class. In private kindergarten and nursery school there was one teacher for every five children, and everyone had received a lot of attention. This was different. I was ready to relate to the teacher but was not sure if she had even noticed me. As time progressed, I made new friends and found it easy enough to learn the required curriculum.

One day when I was in third grade, the teacher announced a special competition, sponsored by an organization in America, for the best fairy tale composed by one of our pupils. The prizes were small celluloid dolls dressed in clothes made from American handkerchiefs. I wrote a story about the life cycle of a raindrop. I can still remember the basic story line.

A raindrop that sat on the petal of a rose evaporated and turned into a mist in the evening hours. The mist changed into a fog that drifted along and after a while turned into a cloud. The raindrop looked down to earth and watched over the rose. Suddenly there came a storm with thunder and lightening, and the raindrop danced back down to earth. She looked for the rose but could not find it. Then once again the raindrop evaporated and turned to mist and went through the cycle over and over again.

This story meant a great deal to me—it was an attempt to handle my loss of Martha—but it did not win a prize. My teacher accused me of copying the story from a book. I was crestfallen to have been accused of such dishonesty. An even greater disappointment was the fact that my teacher, after more than two years of having me in her classroom, did not know me at all. Obviously she had not noticed that I was already an avid reader. Although this teacher did not know me, I enjoyed learning reading, writing, arithmetic, and geography. At the same time, I had abundant resources available outside of school to enrich my basic education—my parents, books, and the city of Vienna.

NOTE

1. The following is a quotation from Nina Sutton's *Bruno Bettelheim: The Other Side of Madness* (New York: Basic Books, 1996), 63. Bruno Bettelheim was a teenager living in Vienna at the time.

"During a wave of shooting, a policeman's horse was hit, bringing the animal down and wounding the policeman in the process. In the wink of an eye, the crowd rushed at the fallen horse, and a sailor finished it off with a knife, encouraging his fellows to help themselves to a cheap roast. The horse was instantly torn to pieces by the crowd, with men and women fighting over the remains. A few minutes later people could be seen running away, clutching still-steaming chunks of meat."

Chapter Two

Vienna before the Nazis

The Vienna I knew in my childhood and early adolescence was safe, well administered, democratic, beautiful, and reasonably tolerant of the different ethnic groups who lived there. It was also rich in culture, still enjoying the revolutionary changes in science and the arts that had begun in the late nineteenth century, during the sixty-five-year-long reign of Emperor Franz Joseph of the Habsburg Empire.

Vienna had been the capital of the Austria-Hungarian Empire with its fifty million inhabitants. With the demise of the Habsburg rule at the end of World War I, the empire was broken up, with Italy, Poland, and Rumania acquiring new territories and Czechoslovakia and Yugoslavia becoming newly formed, independent nations. This left Austria and Hungary drastically reduced in size, population, and resources. No longer the capital of a vast empire, Vienna was now the capital of Austria, a small country with a population of only six and a half million, one third of whom resided in Vienna. In 1919 Austria was declared a republic, and for the first time all adult citizens, both male and female, were given the right to vote.

The Social Democrats defeated the Christian Social Party in the election and stayed in power in Vienna until 1934. Though their municipal administration was often referred to as "Red Vienna," the Social Democrats were not communists like the perpetrators of the Russian Revolution but socialists like their peace-loving counterparts in Scandinavia, bent on building a good and just society for all. They introduced the eight-hour work day, unemployment benefits, and free lectures on cultural endeavors. They built public housing projects, kindergartens, schools, youth centers, libraries, hospitals, and sports facilities. They subsidized education and all the arts, thereby guaranteeing that the cultural renaissance would survive World War I. They raised the money for all these projects not by borrowing but by taxing luxuries such as large private cars, riding horses, hotel rooms, and servants in private house-holds. My parents had to pay a luxury tax for Vettie and Lisa, but I never heard them complain. They were proud to live in a city that John Gunther in *Inside Europe* called "probably the most successful municipality in the world."[1]

FIN DE SIÈCLE

The Fin de Siècle in Austria was a remarkable, comparatively short-lived cultural revolution that started in the late nineteenth century under Franz Joseph and ended when Hitler took over in 1938. During the late nineteenth and early twentieth centuries Vienna was a melting pot. People from all over the empire came to Vienna to find work, to attend schools and universities—thought to be among the best in Europe—and to contribute their energy and diversity to the cultural renaissance. In art, architecture, literature, music, and science, talented people rebelled against static traditions in art, the repressive and hypocritical Victorian culture, and the morally restrictive edicts of the Catholic Church, and set out in exciting new directions.

In art and architecture, it was the beginning of modernism as represented by Art Nouveau, Art Deco Viennese style, Biedermeier constructions, and the Secession Movement, which was founded by the artist Gustav Klimt. The slogan of the Secessionists was *Arbeit macht frei* or "Work liberates" by which they meant the work of artists. The Nazis stole this slogan and put it on the entrance of most concentration camps. All the Secessionist artists were agreed on one point—to make a complete break from the past. Among the iconoclastic writers at the time were Bertolt Brecht, Kurt Weil, Franz Werfel, Arthur Schnitzler, Stephan Zweig, Joseph Roth, Hugo von Hof-mannsthal, and many more. Franz Kafka, a native of Prague rather than Vienna, was considered to be part of the movement and his works were much discussed and widely read. Musically there was Arthur Schoenberg with his atonal music and emphasis on the twelve-tone method of composition. Alban Berg and Anton Weber were two of his most famous students. In science there was Sigmund Freud, educated as a neurologist, who founded the theory and practice of psychoanalysis. He created a sexual revolution through his findings and by his use of the term Eros (the Greek god of love), which he expanded developmentally from infancy on. The work of Freud and his colleagues such as Alfred Adler, Sandor Ferenczi, Otto Rank, Ernest Jones, Karl Abraham, and Carl Jung called into question the Victorian attitude toward sex so prevalent among the Viennese. During my adolescence I was aware of Freud's work and knew people who had been analyzed by Freud's students, but I had no idea of the profound effect his work would have on me and my own work after the war.

CULTURE

Most of the places we wanted to go in Vienna were within walking distance of our house. In school we learned about the history of Vienna and its many impressive buildings, but for the most part I took them for granted because I saw them every day. In warm weather as we strolled along the Ringstrasse, we would often hear Strauss waltzes reverberating from the pavilions in the parks. Haydn, Mozart, Beethoven, Schubert, Brahams, Wagner, Bruckner, Mahler, and Lehar had all lived and worked in Vienna, and their music was part of our everyday life. My parents were culturally very astute and saw to it that I was exposed at an early age to concerts, plays, ballet, art exhibitions, operas, and operettas—all of which I absorbed like a sponge and found just as exciting as riding the Ferris wheel at the Prater or watching the Lipizzaner horses go through their elaborate ballet under crystal chandeliers.

In Vienna in those days grammar schools were conducted from eight in the morning to noon, and high schools from eight to one on weekdays and eight to noon on Saturdays. This gave us time to pursue other activities, even though the homework assigned was extensive.

When I was eight years old, my parents enrolled me in the Vienna Music Conservatory for Children to take piano, dancing, French, and choir singing. Thanks to my parents, I had learned to like new challenges and I loved every minute of my new educational adventure.

My piano teacher was a famous professor by the name of Fuchs who told me that I was very talented but did not practice enough. She wanted me to practice three hours a day, while I, with my homework and other activities, could find time to practice only an hour and a half. Every quarter we performed in piano recitals, with the director of the music school, a man I did not know, acting as conductor. I knew my piece cold and could play it even if you were to wake me up in the middle of the night. But when I saw this strange man conducting my piece, I panicked. My fingers got away from me and I played the piece much too fast. I will never forget the disappointed look on my teacher's face. I was her showpiece, her pride and joy, and I had flubbed up. Fortunately there were other occasions when I made her proud of my technique and what she called "my sensitive and impressionistic" playing.

What I loved most at the Conservatory were the dancing lessons, since I had been trained in this art form. I was always picked to give a solo dance or to be the center in a group of three. We had a famous instructor, Giza Gertz, who later fled to Israel. She worked all of us very hard, especially those of us who were often dancing solo. We undertook many dance recitals, which I thoroughly enjoyed. We performed Spanish, Russian, and Hungarian dances and sometimes danced in full ballets. The one I will never forget is *Cinderella*, performed at the Carlton Theatre. At the beginning of the ballet another girl and I, playing ladies of the court, always entered center stage to do our curtsy to the queen. At the first performance, there was a last-minute change and the two of us were instructed to enter from the right. Having learned my curtsey in a certain way, I had no choice but to turn my behind to the audience. I became a laughing stock, much to my dismay.

FRIENDS

During my childhood and early teens I always had friends to play with, to rely on, and to share my things with. My most vivid memory is of Susie, my closest friend all through kindergarten and grammar school, who lived just two houses down. We saw each other nearly every day and played well together. We were like sisters. At times, Susie was competitive with me and demanded that her parents buy her the same toys I had. My assumption was that she was left to her own devices too much and needed more of her parents' attention. Off and on another friend named Trude joined us, and the three of us would visit the nearby park where we played with the other children, who were mostly boys. The games we played were rough and tough and the boys respected us for our contributions. Occasionally Susie and I would watch a movie or two. Susie's father, a relative of Otto Preminger, was in the film business, and just by mentioning his name, we were allowed to attend movie houses for free.

Each year just before Lent there was a children's ball held in the Secession Building, the museum built in 1897 and dedicated to displaying the work of the Secessionist artists. To this date, it is one of the most innovative and beloved buildings in Vienna, revered for its unique architectural features. I attended the Children's Ball in two consecutive years. The first year a boy called me on the phone and asked if I would dance with him at the ball. I said, "Yes, if you will dance with my friend as well."

When my parents heard about this, they laughed at me. I asked them what was so funny.

"You're so naïve," Mother said.

I did not understand. "I was just practicing Tzedakah, sharing what I have, to make the world a better place—like you and Father are always telling me to do."

"Tzedakah is giving back to the community things like goods and services," she explained with a smile. "You don't have to share your boyfriends."

For the first children's ball I created my own costume. It was a cerise satin dress that I used in my dance classes, short in front and long in back, with large pieces of fabric falling from the arms. Although I wasn't much of a seamstress, I rose to the occasion and lined the hem and the sleeves with golden braid and sewed sodium signs in gold braid all over the costume. I made a pointed hat of the same material as the dress and devised a veil that dangled from the top of the hat nearly to my shoulders. In my hand I carried a black wand and called myself a magician. The costume won second prize. The second year I wore a ready-made costume of Biedermeier style, the dress I had worn for my role as lady of the court in *Cinderella*. The costume consisted of a pink satin dress with crinolines, a silver tiara, and a silver fan. Trude came along dressed very creatively as a wool ball. Neither of us won any prizes but we both had a great time waltzing the night away at this grand occasion.

PREADOLESCENCE AND ADOLESCENCE

At about age nine my friends and I began to wonder about our physical development, the start of secondary characteristics—hair beginning to grow under our arms and in the pubic region and some breast development. When we reached this age, we had not been given any preparation whatsoever. In the repressed Viennese culture and hypocritical society, sex was a taboo subject, talked about neither at home nor at school, nor were there any lessons in biology on the sexuality of animals or even plants. So the three of us—Susie, Trude, and I—shared our knowledge, or lack thereof, regarding the normal human developmental process.

In Susie's flat there was a locked cupboard containing medical dictionaries. Susie managed to find the key and we started to educate ourselves, examining our bodies by comparing signs and symptoms in a very hush-hush manner. We knew we were not supposed to ask questions, but our natural curiosity took over and we examined each other between the legs. Our fantasy was that there was one cloaca and that pregnancy could be achieved by a kiss. Trude, feeling guilty, told her mother of our research. Trude's mother told the other two mothers and all three mothers were appalled. They lectured us and made us feel extremely guilty, but did nothing to clarify our confusion. In spite of the pioneer work of Sigmund Freud, this prudish attitude was still typical of the times, and unfortunately our parents treated us just as their parents had treated them.

When I started to menstruate at age eleven, I thought I was damaged and torn. I finally sought the advice of my mother, who explained to me what the menses were all about. Perhaps the event of my menses touched off feelings she had had as a youngster. In any case, she decided that my briefcase was too heavy for me on "those days" and insisted on carrying it to school for me in spite of her rheumatic heart. I pleaded with her to leave a few blocks before we reached school, afraid that if the other students saw my mother carrying my bag, they would make fun of me. Fortunately she complied. One day Trude's mother informed me that when a girl started the menses, her body was getting ready to have a baby. This news both frightened and alarmed me. I was only eleven, not ready emotionally to hear this and nowhere near ready to become a mother. When I thought about the changes my body was going through, I became depressed. I feared that I had lost the childish part of myself, which I cherished. After some contemplation I came to the conclusion that I would continue to have the childish part within me regardless of my physical development. This made me feel secure and a total person again.

About this time I became friends with Renate, the daughter of close friends of my family. Renate and her parents went on vacations with us to Czechoslovakia. Although she was twelve years my senior, Renate took me with her to her discussion groups, poetry groups, and lectures, greatly expanding my cultural horizons. She was like an older sister to me, and to some degree, she replaced the close relationship I had had with Martha. Renate at that time was in analysis with one of the students of Sigmund Freud.

Another friend with whom I formed a lasting relationship was Ludwig Mann. Ludwig, the son of Thomas Mann the writer, was a German national who visited us on occasions when in Vienna and stayed in our flat for a few days at a time. His parents were divorced and he lived with his mother in Germany. Our friendship lasted through the time when both of us lived in London.

Two other people I became friendly with were our concierge and his wife. The couple had one of the *Schrebergartens,* named after the originator of these gardens, on the outer edge of Vienna where they grew flowers and vegetables. They invited me to stay with them on many weekends, and I thoroughly enjoyed working the land and helping them harvest their fruit and vegetables. My parents trusted the couple to take good care of me and they did.

HIGH SCHOOL

In Austria high school started after four years of grammar school. When children reached age eleven, they took tests that determined what sort of school they would attend. Those with high scores entered a real-gymnasium, an eight-year school where they received a classical education preparing them to enter a university. The last two years of study were equivalent to two years of college in the United States. Students with lower test scores enrolled in schools that provided a general education.

I was admitted to a real-gymnasium called *Schule der Beamten Toechtern,* a small private girls' school for the daughters of state employees. This school was exclusive, and if you were not the daughter of a state employee, it was not enough to have done well on the entrance test. I was admitted because Father was a good friend of an attorney who was employed by the government.

At the new school, I soon found two new friends, and for a time the three of us were inseparable. The headmistress was a middle-aged spinster called Frau Director Degen, who, like most Austrians, remembered the glory days of the Empire and insisted on always being addressed by her full title, no shortcuts permitted. *Degen,* which means *dagger* in German, was an appropriate name for her, given the talent she displayed for enforcing all the rules and regulations. Behind her back, my friends and I preferred to call her The Dragon because of her fierce expression and protruding teeth. The three of us joined other students in some benign revolts. We were not allowed to wear socks to school, only hose. On the day of an important examination we all appeared wearing socks. Needless to say, we had to complete our examination and were not sent home as we had hoped.

The schoolwork was challenging, serious, and often inspiring. My favorite subjects were literature, biology, philosophy, and art. We had an excellent art teacher, and I participated in extracurricular activities organized around the various art forms. Along with Greek and Latin, I studied English, which I practiced with a friend, an American student whose father was a diplomat. Conversing with her helped me to master the language, which came in handy during my years in Great Britain, where I later fled to escape Hitler. The curriculum placed great emphasis on geography, ancient history, and the history of the Orient, with little about Britain, Africa, or the Western Hemisphere. We studied European history also, and the history of Vienna, both with an Austrian slant. We were told that the Central Powers had won World War I, with Germany withdrawing voluntarily. I did not know that we had lost the war until I arrived in London in 1939.

In the Austrian-Hungarian Empire there was no separation of church and state, a situation that continued after the Habsburg regime phased out, and the Catholic religion was taught in all schools, both public and private. Our school had Protestant and Jewish students along with the Catholics, so those religions had to be taught as well. The religious teacher for the Jewish girls was a young and ambitious rabbi who taught us Ancient Hebrew and required us to write grammatically correct essays in this rather difficult language. My father, proficient in Hebrew, was most helpful to me, but all the other Jewish parents complained to the school administration that their children spent so much time struggling with Hebrew that they were neglecting the rest of their studies. Frau Director Degen took notice and modified the curriculum.

All public and private high schools participated in competitive games such as volleyball and soccer, with the winner receiving a prize. I was always chosen as one of the school's representatives in relay running. During the winter months the gymnastics department took students to ski in Mariazell, a well-known resort. My training as a dancer made it easy for me to undertake all sorts of sports activities. Skiing was my favorite.

Where did the pre-adolescents and adolescents hang out? One place we met, both boys and girls, was at a government-sponsored discussion group covering such topics as animal rights, literature, and philosophy. We also hung out at the *Konditoreien*—the pastry shops—where we happily consumed Viennese pastries along with a cup of hot chocolate. Viennese pastries outshone even French pastries in quality and taste. Many people are familiar with Vienna's famous Sacher torte, but I preferred the Dobosh torte with many layers of cake alternating with many layers of chocolate cream, with spun sugar on top. Equally delectable was my mother's vanilla torte which was six or seven inches high with generous amounts of vanilla cream, chocolate cream, mocha cream, strawberry cream, raspberry cream, and pineapple cream between its many layers. Caloric and delicious!

Vienna has always been a hotbed of anti-Semitism, but as a child and young girl in Vienna, I was not its victim, nor was my family. Although most of our friends were Jewish, some were Catholic and Protestant. I did not think much about it. The neighborhood we lived in contained all three groups as did my schools and classes at the Conservatory. I was aware that there were anti-Semitic newspapers in Vienna, and I picked up on an undercurrent of anti-Semitism every Easter when I watched the elaborate processions staged by the Catholic Church on the city's main streets. Along with the incense, the holy water, the choir boys, and the clergy in their magnificent robes, they called attention to Judas's betrayal of Jesus. This, by virtue of highly fallacious reasoning, implied that all Jews everywhere were killers of Christ, an accusation I heard repeated by children at school. Not until much later did I realize that Jesus, Mary, Joseph, and the disciples were also Jews, a point the Austrian Catholics chose to ignore. Another rumor made the rounds in Vienna—that Jews killed Christian babies and drank their blood. I'm not sure where I first heard this malicious fabrication, but it was when I was very young. Possibly Lisa told me as we watched an Easter parade.

During these years no one on the streets ever recognized me as a Jew, perhaps because I looked more like an Aryan than like the stereotypical Jew depicted in cartoons. I had blond hair, a small nose, and gray-green eyes, and I did not wave my arms about, as the stereotype implied. Many Italians talk with their hands and wave their arms but they are not despised for doing it. My family, like most Austrian Jews, did not conform to the stereotype. The only family member that had a crooked nose and a professorial beard was my father.

Although the Nazi party in Austria was fairly small and ineffective during the 1920s, Father, who was politically astute, predicted the Nazis' rise to power in Germany and became noticeably agitated and upset whenever he read or heard about Hitler and his hooligans. In those days people generally did not consider Hitler a serious threat, but laughed at him and thought him crazy.

THE DEATH OF MY FATHER

Father took several business trips a year, mostly to Germany but sometimes to Czechoslovakia. One morning in July 1931 when I was eleven, he and I were sitting over a bowl of cherries before his departure for Germany. In anticipation of his birthday, I had purchased a leather briefcase for him by saving money from my allowance. He ordered a taxi and kissed my mother and me goodbye. An hour later we received a call from the hospital informing us that Father had suffered a heart attack in the taxi en route to the railroad station. The taxi driver drove him to the nearest hospital where he was declared dead on arrival. We were stunned. He had seemed healthy, and we had had no warning signs.

Mother took to her bed and stayed there for many weeks, and for a time it seemed as if I had lost both parents. Mother's severe depression may have been triggered by guilt about the loss of her own father to whom she was devoted. She told me that one day her father had asked her to stay home with him but she, not recognizing that he was gravely ill, had chosen instead to go to her secretarial job. When she returned, he was dead. In one loss, we usually rework previous losses, which gives us some relief, but in my opinion, one can never completely overcome losses—especially sudden losses, which are the most traumatic.

This was such a painful time for me that I have blocked out many of the details. My father had been more than a father to me. He was also a guide, a role model, an ego ideal, and someone to discuss ideas with. Although he was old enough to be my grandfather, he was, above all, my best friend.

Aunt Paula and Uncle Filip began coming to our house every day and joined us for meals. Vettie prepared the meals and continued to take care of the house, but when autumn arrived, the Persian carpets and velvet curtains were still stored away in mothballs and Mother had not left her bed. The house, so cool and airy in summertime, seemed cold and unwelcoming that fall.

According to Jewish tradition, I wore black for six months, black and white for another three months, and ended the mourning period with a black band around my arm. Whereas before I loved to learn, now I could not concentrate. My grades dropped dramatically, and I flunked a history test. The school found me a tutor and the history teacher gave me a second chance, but I failed the exam a second time.

The trauma of my loss also affected me physically. I became anemic and my weight dropped. Our family physician told my mother to feed me raw liver and not to allow me to continue dancing lessons. This deprivation made me even more depressed since for me dancing was a good emotional outlet.

Partly because of her emotional upset, Mother developed high blood pressure. In those days, taking blood from a patient was the accepted remedy, and the doctor took a great deal of blood from Mother, a process which I was allowed to watch. I thought the procedure barbaric—it was like watching the life drain out of her—but much to my surprise, Mother soon got better. By late fall she was back on her feet and had resumed her daily activities.

During the early part of the mourning period I imagined that my father's soul was going to Heaven and that he was watching over me, like a guardian angel. Towards the end of the mourning period I came to the conclusion that the memory of my father was internalized within me. This meant that his emotional and intellectual values became my own, as well as his *Weltanschauung* (worldview). I was a "chip off the old block," a state of mind that could not be taken away from me. This understanding enabled me to get on with my life.

CONCLUDING THE GRIEF WORK

Mother made Uncle Filip my legal guardian, explaining that I needed a father figure to identify with. Uncle Filip was glad to take on this role and loved every minute of it. He invested a great deal of time and energy in me and was very warm, empathetic, and understanding. He introduced me to the Viennese coffee house culture.

Coffee houses were elegant gathering places, distinguished one from the other by the various trades and professions of the patrons who frequented them. A particular coffee house might serve primarily artists or writers or musicians or merchants of various kinds. Uncle Filip frequented a coffee house in the Sixth District where wholesale jewelers did their bartering. Since precious stones could be carried in one's pocket, barter was easily achieved. At the coffee house you could sip a cup of coffee for hours, read newspapers from all over Europe, and receive friends who would sit and chat with you over a glass of water. The waiters, dressed in tuxedos and aprons, would make sure that your water glass was full no matter how long you chose to linger. There were several varieties of coffee to choose from such as black or white, large or small, with or without whipped cream. Sometimes a sandwich or sweet roll was added to the menu. To this day, I cannot understand how these coffee houses could continue to exist, with what must have been a very small margin of profit. Many patrons, most of them men, spent time there, but none of them spent much money.

Because of my low grades, Uncle Filip and Mother decided that I should change schools. My new school, also a girls' school, was a business school. Instead of Greek and Latin I studied typing, shorthand, and how to write a good business letter. I made new friends and gradually regained the ability to concentrate. I became a good student once again, especially enjoying the excellent classes in literature, biology, English, and art.

Except for the dancing lessons, I continued to participate in my usual activities after Father's death, and by the end of the mourning period I had begun to enjoy them again—the piano lessons, the choir, and the French lessons at the Conservatory, the musical evenings at home, and the lectures, concerts, and plays in Vienna. My friends and I could attend the opera inexpensively by purchasing "standing room only" tickets on the ground floor. We would queue up in a long line to buy tickets, only to stand again throughout the performance itself. From our vantage point we got an excellent view of the entire performance, and I attended a vast array of operas with my friends.

Now that Aunt Paula and Uncle Filip were spending so much time with my mother and me, their friends began to visit them at our flat. One day a handsome and charming, serious and cultured young man named Erwin Pollitt came to visit. He had a university degree in engineering. I assumed he had a law degree as well, because he worked for the Austrian government as a patent attorney. I was impressed. He was twenty eight, an adult to look up to, and I was thirteen. Erwin treated me like a little sister, but whenever I heard that he was coming to visit, I made it a point to stay home.

By the time I was fourteen, my girlfriends and I had pooled our scant knowledge of sexual development and were prepared to start dating. On my first date, with a student from the medical school, Mother came along, walking about twenty paces behind us. She must have decided I was trustworthy, because after that she either attended the balls as a chaperone or stayed home. Once she had made it clear that she trusted me, I felt I could trust myself.

Around this same time Mother decided that I was old enough to travel alone to Budapest to visit her cousins. Since I was still a minor, I was included on my mother's passport, which meant she had to accompany me to the border. Because of the strained relations between Czechoslovakia and Hungary, Mother, who had a Czech passport, was often bodily searched, even though she spoke fluent Hungarian. These visits to Budapest were good for me. They made me feel more self-confident. My cousin László was a professional pianist who practiced six hours a day. I was in awe of his technique and dedication. A highlight of my visits to Hungary was a folk festival that took place every summer. Peasants from all over Hungary appeared in their local costume to dance their particular version of the csárdás. In the evening everyone had a chance to dance—not the Viennese waltz but the Hungarian folk dances I had learned in my classes at the Conservatory—and I was passed from one man to another without a break.

Increasing my circle of friends, I started to join youth groups sponsored by the Social Democratic Party. Our main activity was hiking. After attending a ball that ended early in the morning, I would go home, catch two or three hours' sleep, and get up at five o'clock to pack food in my rucksack and meet the "gang" at six at the train station. We would travel out to the Vienna Woods or to a village in the mountains and spend the day hiking. It is hard for me now to imagine that I had enough energy to stay up half the night dancing only to go hiking for the whole of the following day.

By the time I reached my late teens, I was a relatively happy and well adjusted young woman. I had come to terms with the loss of Martha. Although the tragic death of my father left a burning gap in my life, I knew that he would stay within me and I recognized that I was blessed to have had him as long as I did. At this point in my life I was proud to be a Jew. My family, especially my father, had instilled in me a respect for the Jewish religion, and I was aware of what a prominent role Jews had played in the life of Vienna, culturally, scientifically, intellectually, economically, and politically. At the same time, I was proud to be an Austrian. I loved the mountainous countryside and Vienna with its exciting cultural and social life, and I admired the Social Democrats whose enlightened social policies had implanted in me a lasting idealism. I felt confident that my life would develop along the lines of my family's expectations for me, which were similar to my own.

In 1938 the medical school ball, elaborate and well attended, was the last ball of the pre-Lent season. My friends and I had waltzed all night long and had a grand time. At four o'clock in the morning of March 11 we were walking west along the Mariahilfer Strasse towards my home in the District of Neubau. Formality was the accepted style in Vienna society, and I can still remember what I was wearing—a light blue silk ball gown with a small trail at the back, white kid gloves extending over my elbows, and Mother's beautiful black seal coat with a colorful art deco lining. The coat was too large for me and hung around my shoulders like a cape.

Suddenly, cutting through the beauty of the night, there came the sounds of adolescent boys singing Nazi songs and intermittently crying "Heil Hitler!" On they came—a band of Hitler Youth marching toward us from the Westbahnhof, the west train station. They were dressed in the Austrian and Bavarian costume associated with the Nazis—shiny Tyrolean leather shorts, off-white hand-knit knee socks, and Loden green Tyrolean hats decorated with edelweiss, Hitler's favorite flower. They marched as one body, with the precision of a machine. My friends and I were horrified. A cold shudder went down my spine and I knew then and there that this was a harbinger of what was to come—the end of civilized life as I had known it.

NOTE

1. John Gunther, *Inside Europe* (New York: Harper & Brothers, 1937) 280.

Chapter Three

Anschluss

On March 11, 1938, the Austrian Nazi Party, at the instigation of Hitler and his henchmen, took over Austria's government, and Nazi flags with their black swastikas appeared as if from nowhere on all public places and most private homes. Our concierge, who I had thought was my friend, was the first in our neighborhood to display the Nazi flag and sport a Nazi armband. The following day Austria was officially annexed into the German Third Reich.

On March 15 Hitler came to town and gave a rousing speech from the Heldenplatz (Place of Heroes) to the accompaniment of a military band, marching soldiers, soldiers on horseback, tanks on parade, fighter planes overhead, fireworks, and Sieg Heils from the huge crowd of ecstatic Vienna citizens, who acted as if this day was the high point of their lives.

Less than a month later, on April 10, a plebiscite showed 99.7 per cent of the voters were in favor of Anschluss. To accomplish this, the Nazis had declared that Jews and others unsympathetic to their cause were ineligible to vote. They had also launched a huge propaganda campaign glorifying the so-called Master Race, had convinced the many unemployed workers that the Nazis would provide them with jobs, and had made clear to everyone that their names would be put on a list if they voted No.

My family and I were appalled to think that such a disaster could befall a city that had so recently been a center of civilized society. Until then, I must have repressed any awareness of the economic turmoil, the boiling anti-Semitism, the rise of a fifth column, and the not-so-gradual increase in violent confrontation between political parties.

PAVING THE WAY FOR HITLER

Nazism flourished best in a society like Austria that was already strongly anti-Semitic. During the Middle Ages the Catholic Church did not allow its faithful to lend money and charge interest, so the task was delegated to the Jews, whose religion did not forbid this activity. Nobody loves a usurer, least of all the people who owe him money. Later, when moneylending was mostly the province of banks, people resented the bankers, many of whom were Jews. The official religion of the Habsburg Empire, and later of Austria, was Catholicism, and many Catholics blamed the Jews for killing Jesus. Although the Jews under Kaiser Franz Joseph were granted full citizenship along with freedom of religion, two key politicians were virulently anti-Semitic. One was Georg Ritter von Schönerer, the founder of the pan-German party and a powerful figure in Austria's parliament, who blamed the Jews for everything wrong with society. In 1888, on a drunken rampage, he raided the office of a Jewish-owned newspaper and beat up the editor and members of the staff. Even though he served a brief prison term for this, his popularity rose sharply among his anti-Semitic constituents. The other important anti-Semitic politician was Karl Lüger, the founder of the Christian Social Party. He discovered that anti-Semitic rhetoric won him votes among the petty bourgeoisie who believed that the Jews were "stealing" jobs that should have been theirs. The young Adolf Hitler, living in a homeless shelter in the Vienna slums and taking his meals at a soup kitchen run by nuns, admired Schönerer and Lueger inordinately and found their vitriolic anti-Semitism perfectly suited to his own burgeoning ideology.

In economic hard times people look for a scapegoat, and in Austria the scapegoat has usually been the Jews. In the early 1920s there was rampant inflation, and currency lost its value from one day to the next. Employees asked for their daily salaries to make sure they would be able to buy groceries. One summer when our family was vacationing by the North Sea, Father telephoned Mother and urgently told her to spend all the money she had with her because the following day it would be worth next to nothing. Printing presses worked night and day, churning out paper money so fast that sometimes the bills were only printed on one side. During my sojourn in Germany after World War II, I came across some of these one-sided bills in one thousand, one million, and ten million mark denominations. They are collectors' items today, but in their time they were worth almost nothing. Austria's shillings underwent the same devaluation, and people lost fortunes overnight. Many Viennese blamed the government for this and, by extension, the Jews, who held prominent positions in the Social Democrat party.

In 1931 the collapse of the Austrian *Creditanstalt*—the largest bank in Europe, owned by the Rothschild family—provoked a financial panic and almost single-handedly brought the Great Depression to Europe. The Austrian Nazi Party, a small group until then, was able to double its membership every year. More prosperous Austrians dealt with the crisis in typical Austrian fashion—denial. Frederic Morton reported in the *New York Times* that during the carnival season that year "red ink seemed to be just another festive color."[1]

When the Social Democrats were in power in Vienna during the 1920s and early 1930s, anti-Semitism was very much alive in the Christian Social Party whose strength lay in the countryside where people tended to be conservative, Catholic, relatively poor, and jealous of their richer fellow countrymen in Vienna. In 1934 in Vienna there was a bloody confrontation between the Social Democrats and the federal government, then headed by Chancellor Engelbert Dollfuss, the leader of the Christian Social Party. Dollfuss was determined to remove the Social Democrats from power, and he succeeded, with the battleground being the housing complexes of the workers. The poorly armed leftist forces were no match for the army and eventually surrendered. Otto Bauer, the Jewish leader of the Social Democrats, fled to Czechoslovakia. The Left was no longer in a position to resist Fascism in any of its forms.

On July 25, 1934, Dollfuss, one kind of Fascist, was murdered in the *Bundeskanzleramt*, the seat of the federal government, by another kind of Fascist—the Austrian Nazis. The conspirators were a well-disciplined group made up of officers of the Vienna police and former soldiers of the Austrian army who had been dismissed because of their Nazi sympathies. Hitler backed the putsch but did not support it once Dollfuss was dead and the conspirators' plans went astray. Dr. Kurt von Schuschnigg took over as Chancellor, opposing unification with Germany with all the power he could muster. In March 1938, however, he succumbed to Hitler's threat of force, knowing that the Austrian army was no match for superior German forces.

VIENNA UNDER THE NAZIS

On the second day of the Anschluss three SA troopers, Brown Shirts, rang our bell. I went to the door, looked through the peephole, and saw three hooligans, the dregs of society. "Ausmachen!" one of them shouted, a rude command to open the door. My heart stopped beating. I secured the chain lock and opened the door as far the chain permitted. The thugs clicked their heels together and greeted me with a snappy "Heil Hitler." I did not *Heil Hitler* them back. By this time Mother had joined me. Without removing the chain lock, we explained that we were foreigners—citizens of Czechoslovakia. To our astonishment, these gangster types actually listened. Instead of leading us away, they redirected their energies and proceeded to march up one floor and arrest our neighbor, an Aryan, that is, a pure non-Jewish Christian with no Jewish ancestors. The reason for this arrest was *Rassenschande* (Shame of the Race), because he had a Jewish girlfriend. The brutes beat him, then sent him to a concentration camp where he died.

Ottakring, the Thirteenth District where the underclass resided, one of Hitler's stomping grounds in his homeless days, was the district with the highest unemployment, delinquency, and crime rate in Vienna. This is where much of the recruitment for the Austrian Nazi Party took place. Recruits were indeed plentiful. All the disenfranchised youth and underworld characters suddenly sported the Nazi uniform of the SA and proceeded to take out their long-seething rage upon the Jewish population of Vienna. Their hatred for the Jews had no boundaries, nor did the projections of their own deprivations know any limits. This same enthusiasm for the Nazi party was manifested in other parts of Vienna as well. The sneering and simmering anti-Semitism was openly accepted and enacted by the police, by other government employees, and by many middle class Viennese who considered themselves good citizens.

The Austrian thugs were much more brutal than their German counterparts. Because they had been illegal in Austria for several years, they went wild. Thomas Weyr in *The Setting of the Pearl: Vienna under Hitler* describes it like this:

> Clearly, coming to power at last had unleashed all the bloodlust Austrian Nazis had accumulated during their years underground. Torturing Jews, physically and psychologically, became a public spectacle as Austrian Nazis were no longer constrained by the more verbal than physical anti-Semitism that had been the Austrian norm. [2]

Random acts of sadism were everywhere. The Hitler Youth beat up their Jewish schoolmates, the Brown Shirts raided coffee houses, charged into the homes of Jews to beat them up and smash their possessions, and took over Jewish-owned stores, dragging the owners out to the street to beat them or shoot them or send them off to concentration camps. On several occasions I witnessed with horror the burning of books in huge bonfires in the street. Uniformed Nazis were gleefully destroying books by Jewish authors and everyone else whose ideas did not conform to the official Nazi doctrine. It was as if the Nazis were trying to wipe out creativity and rational thought forever.

Almost immediately after the Anschluss Jews in prominent positions in businesses, government, theaters, museums, schools, universities, the Opera, the Vienna Philharmonic, and the Music Conservatory were fired and replaced by Nazis. Erwin Pollitt, our family friend, lost his position as a patent attorney working for the government and started a wool business, trading with Scotland and Great Britain so that he could keep his income in the United Kingdom, anticipating ultimate emigration to the United States. My friend Renate, who was studying law at the Vienna University was beaten and literally thrown out by her "fellow" Nazi students simply because she was Jewish. Her boyfriend Max, also Jewish, was ousted by the Nazis from his position as teacher of literature and history in a real-gymnasium. Jewish students were no longer permitted to attend schools such as the real-gymnasium that I had attended after completing grammar school.

Soon Jews were banned from their professional organizations, banned from public swimming pools, banned from the Prater, not allowed to drive cars or possess jewelry of any kind. My family took our jewelry and hid it in a pot of fat. Those Jews who had luggage locks made of platinum or gold as a way to take something of value out of the country were soon discovered and punished. If more than three Jews were found together in a public place, they were treated as a conspiracy and were arrested, beaten, and sent to concentration camps. It was unsafe to be seen in public without a swastika on your lapel. The solution for my mother and me was to wear the Czech flag in place of a swastika. Uncle Filip, an Austrian citizen, was left unmolested for a while and so was Aunt Paula, who was stateless. Fortunately for them, they looked like Aryans. One of my mother's cousins was not so lucky. Shortly after the Anschluss the Nazis took over his real estate business and arrested the entire family, sending them to Bergen-Belsen where they perished.

Another of Mother's cousins, Arthur Brauch, a doctor in chemistry who owned a pharmaceutical factory in Vienna, was treated differently. His company had contracts with businesses all over Europe, but after the Anschluss, these contracts were regarded as null and void. The Nazis informed him that he could leave Austria and take his belongings with him, provided that he would ask each of the businesses to continue their contractual agreement. Uncle Filip, at the risk of his own life, provided jewelry for him so that he could take his assets out of the country. A group of Brown Shirts escorted him and his family to the airport and ushered them onto the plane. Needless to say, my cousin did not renew anybody's contract. Instead he flew with his wife and two daughters to London.

We lived in a paranoid society. Anyone who had a beef or negative feeling about someone else could take out their rage in the streets. Whenever one person pointed at another person and shouted that he or she had said something negative about the Führer, the accused was instantly beaten, arrested, and thrown into prison. I witnessed this on three occasions. As a result, innocent people were constantly looking over their shoulder to see if someone was pointing a finger at them. Once I was stopped by two Storm Troopers and ordered to hold a sign that read, "Don't buy from Jews." I complied. If I had refused, I would have been beaten and thrown into prison.

The sudden takeover by the Nazis changed the entire conception one had of oneself. The Jews, who had been thriving and fully integrated into Austrian life, were now the underclass, an undesirable element, an unwanted society. Hitler's ultimate goal, well documented in *Mein Kampf*, was to exterminate them in order to purify the Aryan race. One suddenly felt like a hunted and haunted deer, without the right to exist. I saw a group of Jews forced to get down on their knees and eat grass, at the whim of a Nazi officer. Others were forced to clean the pavement with toothbrushes as the Hitler Youth stood by. The German language lends itself to perfunctory commands which we heard whenever Jews were being humiliated and abused. "Verboten!" was used to inform Jews of all the things they were not allowed to do, and the dreaded word "Heraus!" meaning "Outside!" was used to throw them out of their businesses and their homes. What was especially discouraging to me was that crowds of Austrian citizens always gathered around to watch the abuse with great sadistic delight, sneering and laughing and encouraging the mistreatment.[3]

I still had a few normal activities in my life at this time. Uncle Filip found me a job tutoring preadolescent boys in their homes. These boys had been neglected by their parents, who were rarely at home, and consequently had serious learning problems. They gained a lot from the attention I was able to give them, and it was gratifying to me to watch their progress. I was also asked to see Gerda, a former schoolmate of mine whose mother had committed suicide. I visited her several times a week in an attempt to reinforce her wish to go on living. Gerda, an accomplished violinist, kept playing the violin for me, partly to soothe herself. Because my own sister had committed suicide, it was easy for me to empathize with Gerda and understand what she was going through. These early experiences in helping troubled young people gave my life a direction that ultimately led to my becoming a child therapist.

KRISTALLNACHT

Hitler and his henchmen needed more money to support their new armaments program. They had already spent all the Jewish assets they had seized. When a Jewish teenager shot an official at the German embassy in Paris, the Nazis used this as a pretext to launch violent anti-Jewish pogroms throughout Germany, Austria, and the Sudetenland. In Vienna, on November 10, 1938, in a carefully planned exercise, they burned and ravaged all but one of the synagogues and Jewish prayer houses, kicked out approximately two thousands Jews from their homes, and destroyed more than four thousand Jewish-owned businesses. Some Jews were killed, many were injured, and more than four thousand were beaten and sent to Dachau concentration camp. This unprecedented and brutal action revealed the deep, primitive, and irrational hatred toward the Jews. The beasts were in command.

All that day and night we stayed home for safety reasons, and not until the next day did we see the devastation—broken glass strewn all over the streets and gaping, empty shop windows without merchandise. It looked as if an especially virulent cyclone had targeted the streets of Vienna, but this one was manmade. The events of this day were so violent and scandalous that it hurt the prestige of the Nazi party. From the Nazis' point of view, however, the pogrom was a success. It enriched their coffers, and it banished more Jews from participation in Vienna society.

PLANS TO EMIGRATE

The day after Kristallnacht Uncle Filip wrote to one of his American friends and asked him to sponsor my emigration to the United States. His friend agreed and sent me an affidavit to come to Portland, Oregon. Jewish emigration was one activity the Nazis encouraged, but given the turn of events, the Austrian quotas determined by the United States government were oversubscribed and I was put on a waiting list. I used this time to get my papers in order. I needed the police record, a tax statement, and several other documents. There were many people like me who were eager to emigrate and were going through the same steps. We had to pick up the papers and documents at the once elegant Rothschild Estate. We arrived before dawn and stood in line for hours with the SS standing guard. They pushed us around and poked their guns into our ribs. When the offices opened at nine o'clock, a cold and tired crowd drifted in to rooms stripped bare of all their former treasures. Paintings, statues, furniture, and books—all had been packed up and sold to help finance the Nazis' war machine.

While waiting for a possible visa to the United States, I completed a course on how to be a nursery school teacher, with an emphasis on the Montessori methods. I enjoyed this course immensely, and it came in handy for me later, during my years in England.

One day a labor permit arrived by mail from London. To this day, I have no idea who sent it to me. The British had great trouble finding domestic servants in those days because they paid them poorly and treated them badly. Since they were unable to obtain British servants, they opened their doors to domestic servants from abroad. For me the labor permit was a kind of insurance, but I still hoped that my American visa would come through.

NOTES

1. Frederic Morton, "The Armageddon Waltz," *New York Times* Mar. 8 2009: WK12.

2. Thomas Weyr, *The Setting of the Pearl: Vienna Under Hitler* (Oxford: Oxford University Press, 2005) 78-9.

3. In Sarah Gainham's book *The Habsburg Twilight: Tales From Vienna*, between pages 148 and 149 she inserts two pages of photos to illustrate her points. On the second page of this photo display are depicted two ultra-Orthodox Jews in their religious garb. The caption reads "Vienna Jews." I take great objection to this misleading description of the Jews in Vienna of whom I am one. This is a misrepresentation of the facts. In the Second District of Vienna there was a large community of Jews of different denominations. I, however, having lived in Vienna during my childhood and adolescence and having traveled around the city a great deal, never came across even one Orthodox Jew. There may have been a few, but they certainly were not representative of the Jewish community, just the reverse. Most Viennese Jews had identified with their cultural surroundings and viewed themselves as Austrians first and as Jews second. They were acculturated and upright citizens contributing economically and culturally to their community.

It is interesting to note that the Orthodox Jews in Vienna were used as scapegoats for the anti-Semitism of the Austrians. During the Nazi uprising, these feelings were displaced and projected onto all the Jews. Many Austrians blame the Nazi uprising and the general disdain for Jews on the few Orthodox Jews who were carving out their place in Vienna in order to make a living. Most of them came from Eastern European countries such as Poland and Hungary. Their manner of dressing and their hairstyles stood out from the rest of society and therefore represented a threat. I don't recall that a person dressed in a Persian outfit with a turban was a threat to the Viennese. In other words, the so-called threat of the Orthodox Jews was race based.

Chapter Four

On My Own in London

Thanks to the man from the Joint Distribution Committee who bought me a ticket at the Dutch border, I took the train to Hoek van Holland and caught the ferry to England. My Czech passport worked at the English border, and when I arrived at the train station in London, I was met by my old friend Ludwig Mann, who had been waiting for me for hours. That we met in London was by design. Mother had sent him a telegram telling him the approximate time of my arrival. Ludwig carried my heavy suitcase to a place in Bloomsbury that provided temporary shelter for refugees. Volunteers provided soup and sandwiches, my first meal since leaving Vienna.

Ludwig and a host of political refugees lived in a large house complete with secret passages on an estate in Wimbledon. His mother, whom I knew from Vienna, was politically active against Hitler's regime and advocated war against Germany. She once participated in a political demonstration in the United States, but since foreigners were not entitled to participate in such events, she was sent back to Germany.

The shelter in Bloomsbury had an employment bureau that found me a job as the companion to an elderly Lady who wanted to brush up on her German. She found me a room in a boarding house across the street and had me converse with her every day, speaking only in German. Although the job did not give me an opportunity to improve my English, it served as an introduction to English mores. Everything seemed so different from the Viennese way of doing things. This job was not bad—my employer was pleasant enough—but it did not last long. The British authorities reminded the Lady that foreign workers were required to live on the premises so that the authorities could keep track of them. The Lady had a son, the chief social worker at a hospital, who still lived with her, and she felt it would be inappropriate for me to live in the same house with him. Forced to leave, I returned to the refugee house.

One day a stately woman arrived at the employment bureau holding a lorgnette through which she peered. Everyone bowed down and treated her with the utmost respect. Someone pointed a finger at me, and after she had thoroughly looked me over, like a piece of merchandise, she chose me for a position about which I was not informed. In the car, a Rolls Royce, I sat next to the chauffeur while she interviewed me through her sliding glass window.

SCULLERY MAID

The Honorable Lady Norton lived alone in a four-story Victorian house in Mayfair on Charles Street just off Berkeley Square. The house was large— destined to be turned into an American Red Cross Club after the war. Lady Norton had six servants. There was a cook who did nothing but cook, a personal maid who took care of Lady Norton's social calendar and correspondence, a parlor maid who did nothing but clean the parlor, a general maid, a butler, and a scullery maid. The scullery maid's assignment was to wash dishes, clean vegetables, prepare food for cooking, clean the very large kitchen and hall, make ice cream, clean the maids' rooms, and do many other menial tasks. I was the scullery maid, the servant of the servants, the last to be served at the dinner table, the lowest of the low. The servants modeled the bad treatment they received from their employer in their dealings with me. Although I found myself living in a free country, my duties left me almost no time or energy to meet people or explore the city. One time on my half day off I traveled all the way to Wimbledon to meet Ludwig, and once he traveled to Mayfair to visit me, but then we drifted apart and did not see each other again. Later he married an English woman ten years his senior.

Before the war started with its accompanying food shortages, Lady Norton gave many elaborate dinner parties, serving seven courses of the best and finest food, quite different from the food that was fed to her staff. She frequently entertained royal guests, including the King and Queen. I was hoping to catch a glimpse of them but never did. Although I helped put their food onto platters, the platters were carried up to the dining room on a silent butler. Lady Norton was sometimes critical of her guests. If people consumed more than two of her little new potatoes, she called them hogs. She often came to the kitchen and, peering through her lorgnette, inspected the plates, which were stacked on a huge plate stand that took up three quarters of the room.

Lady Norton's house was lavishly and tastefully furnished. Persian carpets were spread over parquet floors, crystal chandeliers hung in the wings, and every piece of furniture was a precious antique. Well-chosen paintings and art objects lent the finishing touches. The effect was rather like the interior of Buckingham Palace. What struck me most was her dressing-room/bathroom combination. The bathtub, which was octagonal, resided in the middle of the room. Lady Norton's wardrobe lay behind the walls and hidden doors, and all the walls and doors were covered with mirrors, the ultimate display of narcissism.

The servants' quarters differed dramatically from Lady Norton's rooms. My room was located at the top of the house and had a slanting ceiling. There was a bed, a beat-up chest of drawers, a chair, and a table. Three two-by-fours nailed to the wall comprised my wardrobe which was too small to accommodate the few clothes I had brought with me. Most of my clothes I kept in my suitcase and took them out as needed. The other servants' rooms, down the stairs from me, were somewhat better appointed, and the cook's room, in the basement, was large and well furnished, probably organized by the cook herself, who was a Scottish woman. When no one else was around, she treated me much more kindly than the other servants did.

Mother and I had been exchanging frequent long letters ever since I arrived in London. Her letters were a lifeline that kept me going. I was the family representative, the one who had a chance for a decent future, no matter how miserable the present might be. Mother read all my letters to family and friends. In one letter she informed me, in neutral words which got past the censor, that Uncle Filip and Aunt Paula had moved in with her. I assumed that the Nazis had thrown them out of their apartment.

In another letter Mother told me that she had sent my entire dowry to London. She and Aunt Paula had been accumulating the dowry for years. It included napkins, tablecloths, curtains, bedspreads, towels, sheets, and pillowcases, most of which were decorated with Aunt Paula's beautiful blue satin embroidery. Mother packed all this—along with the complete works of Goethe, Schiller, Heine, Mörike, and Shakespeare—into a large crate and sent it off, no doubt to keep it from being stolen by the Nazis. Lady Norton agreed to store the crate somewhere on her premises, but when the crate arrived, she refused to accept it. Her personal maid had warned her not to take it in because she thought I might be a spy. On the advice of the delivery agent, I had the crate sent to a warehouse in the City of London. Later, German incendiary bombs aimed at the City burned down many commercial buildings and my crate along with it. After paying rent for several months for storage, I lost everything. The only proof I had of the contents was a list my mother had sent me. This did not impress the authorities, and my reimbursement was pitifully small.

Lady Norton traveled to Paris in the spring, to Scotland in the fall, and to Nassau in the winter. When sojourning in Scotland, she closed down the house and gave a vacation to all the servants except me. I was instructed to wash the walls, do some extra cleaning, and, most importantly, take care of her Pekinese dog. The dog's meals were delivered every day by the butcher, whereas I had to go out and purchase my meals with my pathetically small salary. Lady Norton insisted that I write to her frequently, keeping her abreast of the dog's eating and elimination habits. Irksome as these duties were, at least I felt that she trusted me, since I was the only caretaker of her house.

When the war broke out, Lady Norton left for France where she was eventually put into a concentration camp. I never found out whether or not she was Jewish or a spy. Perhaps she was both.

FOREIGNERS

During the years preceding World War II, Great Britain had very few foreigners in their midst and *foreigner* was used as a swear word. It meant someone strange and unknown, someone to be ignored and rejected, someone inferior who did not belong, someone who threatened the status quo. It was a relief for me to be in a country where anti-Semitism was not blatantly in evidence, but now I was reviled for being foreign. The people I worked with often called me a "bloody foreigner" and asked, "Why don't you go back where you came from?" In those days many British people were ignorant of geography, history, and political events beyond the confines of their island. I was asked what country Vienna was the capital of and whether Kaiser Franz Joseph, the former emperor of the long defunct Austrian-Hungarian Empire, was still alive. Many of the better educated British extended their knowledge to include the British Empire and, even though the empire was beginning to fall apart, considered themselves superior to everybody everywhere. An upper level Naval officer who became a friend of mine later said, and I quote, "The Germans think they're better than anyone else, but we know that we are."

SOCIAL CLASSES

Before World War II Great Britain was very class conscious. People were judged by their accent, which revealed their social class. Those who attended an exclusive public school, which in reality was a private school, spoke with an accent that was distinctly, clearly, and specifically upper class. Their accent, highly valued in British society, was easily distinguished from the accent of people attempting to emulate it, who sounded forced and unnatural.

The second type of stratification in London society depended on geography. Someone who lived in an upper-class district such as Mayfair, Knightsbridge, or Chelsea was regarded as a person of importance even if he lived in a dingy rented room. On the other hand, someone who lived in a working-class district such as Nottingham, Camden Town, or Tottenham was considered a nonentity and unfit for British society, even if he lived in a mansion.

An upper-class couple I knew from Vienna were victims of this extreme snobbery. Being Jewish, they had been forced to flee the Nazis and leave their assets behind. Like me, they had received labor permits to do domestic service in Great Britain. Before the Anschluss they had spent their winters in Davos, Switzerland, a fashionable ski resort where they befriended an English couple who also vacationed there. The Austrian couple had a standing invitation from their English friends to visit should they ever travel to London. When the Austrians arrived in London, they phoned their English friends who invited them to a dinner party. With the last fifteen shillings she had earned, my friend bought an orchid to wear in her lapel. They were enjoying a pleasant evening dining and exchanging memories when the lady of the house asked them what they were doing in London. The couple explained why they had to flee Austria and come to London to work as a butler and a maid. This news was greeted not with sympathetic shock as one might expect but with silence. Finally the lady of the house spoke up and asked them to leave. The English couple and their upper-class guests could not be expected to sit at the table with servants.

BOARDING HOUSE MAID

"Bloody foreigner! Why don't you go back where you came from?" These words were repeatedly hurled at me by Mrs. Brown, the angry woman who had hired me after Lady Norton left for France.

My new position, that of the only maid in a four-story Georgian-style boarding house near Russell Square in Bloomsbury, required that I wear a black dress with a frilly white organza apron and matching headgear. I lived in a scantily furnished room in the basement and my duties were many. I had to clean the kitchen, the bathrooms, and all ten of the rented rooms without the labor-saving devices we have these days. I also had to serve the tenants both breakfast and morning tea, which meant running up and down the stairs many times each day.

Mrs. Brown, soft-spoken and courteous to the tenants, bullied her husband, a meek little bank clerk, and projected her hate, anxiety, and various misconceptions onto me. She did not fire me—where else could she find a hard worker for fifteen shillings a week?—but she took my rationing book and used my coupons for herself and her husband. Instead of getting my weekly ration of two ounces of butter, two rashers of bacon, two lamb chops, and one egg (if available), along with a monthly can of salmon, I was given a steady diet of stale bread and cheese. To make sure I did not get into her food supply, she kept the cupboard doors locked.

Once the war broke out, letters from home became a source of frustration. We could no longer communicate as we had before because Mother lived in enemy territory. We corresponded exclusively through the Red Cross, whose rules allowed us to use just a few carefully counted words.

There were only two good things in my life at this time. One was conversing with the tenants, most of whom were students at the nearby London University. We huddled around the radio and listened to Mr. Churchill and news of the war. The students treated me as an equal. If Mrs. Brown had known, she would not have allowed it. The other good thing was my half day off every week. On that day I took my meager salary, minus the coins I had to feed to Mrs. Brown's meter whenever I took a bath, and frequented restaurants where I satisfied my hunger. This was very therapeutic, since I was served my food for a change instead of being the servant. In this way I maintained a sense of dignity and self-respect.

During my time at the boarding house I had to appear before a tribunal. Since I had been born in Vienna, the British authorities regarded me as an enemy alien. That I was Jewish and therefore not likely to be a Nazi sympathizer was not taken into consideration. I felt quite anxious before I had to appear. A group of unaccompanied German Jewish teenagers had recently been pulled out of their British high school simply because they were German and were interned on the Isle of Wight. Although I managed to answer the questions to the satisfaction of the officials in charge, I felt as if the whole world was against me. I wanted to leave Mrs. Brown and her boarding house and find another position somewhere else, but I was afraid to try. As an enemy alien, I lacked bargaining power and my next job might be even worse.

Then one day I received a cryptic note from Mother informing me that Erwin Pollitt was on his way to London where he planned to stay until his American visa came through. I was elated. Erwin would tell me what was really going on in Vienna, and he would understand what I was going through and sympathize.

Erwin arrived bearing gifts from Mother—money in English pounds, a beautiful mohair cardigan knitted by Aunt Paula, Austrian bread, Swiss cheese, Belgian chocolates filled with liqueur, anchovy paste in a tube (my favorite), and a huge Hungarian salami about two feet long which was so well cured that it did not have to be refrigerated. I hung the salami from a nail in my room and shared it with Erwin. When he first arrived, I did not have much time to spend with him, but I helped him with his English, which he was studying at the rate of five new words a day, and I showed him around the city. Erwin did not have a work permit and had no idea how long it would take before his American visa came through, so he could not spend much money. He found an inexpensive room in Hampstead Heath, a beautiful, open part of London where many refugees were staying. When I asked him about my family, he tried not to worry me but he did say that the Nazis had taken over Uncle Filip and Aunt Paula's apartment and had thrown them out with just the clothes on their backs.

One evening when I was conversing with some of the students at the boarding house, the warning siren sounded. This was a common occurrence that we usually tried to ignore, but suddenly the whole house started to shake. In their panic and confusion the students tried to push me into a closet to keep me safe, an action I managed to resist. Soon an air raid warden came to the door and told us that a large time bomb had landed in the back yard of our building. Since no one knew when it would explode, we were to pack our things and evacuate the building immediately. My suitcase was ready to go. I had had a premonition of danger and had packed it the night before. It took ten days for the time bomb to be dug out from the backyard, moved to Bloomsbury Square, and exploded by the expert bomb diffusion team.

I spent one night in a public air raid shelter and then found an inexpensive room in Hampstead Heath not far from Erwin. I managed to get a new ration book since Mrs. Brown was still using mine, and we feasted on canned pineapple and lamb stew that I cooked on the gas ring in my room. Erwin's view of me was changing. Our age difference had shrunk considerably, and he no longer thought of me as a child.

For me Erwin's presence was a blessing. He represented the culture into which I was born and reared, and his knowledge of my family had great meaning for me. His warm and giving demeanor, his intelligence, and his empathetic attitude towards me deepened our relationship. He was the anchor I needed emotionally and psychologically in order to survive in the demeaning, deprecating, withholding, and cruel environment in which I found myself.

With Erwin's encouragement, I did not return to the boarding house. Since the bomb had landed in the backyard, there was a great deal of cleanup work I would be asked to do, and it was more than I was willing to handle. My failure to appear at the house represented an acting out of hostility on my part—exactly what Mrs. Brown deserved.

NANNY

The employment bureau at the refugee center found me a job working as a nanny for Sammy, the eighteen-month-old son of a British couple who were Jewish. The family lived in a tastefully furnished basement apartment in a modern building. In wartime London, basement apartments were expensive since they were thought to be safer and more secure than apartments above ground.

This position was an improvement over the last two. My room was better, my salary was better, baby-sitting was for the most part enjoyable, and I had an entire day off each week, which meant I could start to make friends and explore the city. Best of all, Sammy's parents treated me with respect and consideration. It was the first time since my arrival in Great Britain that I had been treated like a human being, and it made a great difference in my ability to function as a unique individual.

My job was to take care of the baby, although there was no structure provided for him. The mother, who was severely depressed for reasons I did not inquire into, slept all day and most of the night. The father played the saxophone with a band in a nightclub. When he came home at four in the morning, he would awaken them both so that Sammy could spend some quality time with his mother, who showered both him and her husband with affection. Compared to most people's schedule, theirs was way out of whack. The father awoke around noon, took care of his son, and did all the shopping, cooking, and laundry. He was mother, father, housekeeper, and breadwinner to his family, and by the time I arrived on the scene, he was physically and emotionally exhausted.

Sammy was a cute, anxious, sensitive baby who presented a challenge for me. I fed him, diapered him, bathed him, played with him, and took him out for long walks in his collapsible baby carriage. Sammy took to me like a fish to water and became much more alert and responsive. He smiled more and sometimes even laughed.

Sometimes Sammy and I rode the Underground to Hampstead Heath to visit Erwin. We would walk and talk and push Sammy in his carriage and enjoy the clean air and open fields. Erwin and I had grown very close. Our friendship had turned into a love relationship we had not originally bargained for. When his visa finally came through, he wanted to marry me and take me with him to America. I wanted to marry Erwin, yet something made me hold back. I asked myself if I was mature enough to get married and if I was ready to give up my hard-earned freedom. I felt that I needed to make something of myself on my own, in part for the sake of my family. The experiences I had had as a maid had something to do with my decision. I had been over-controlled and needed time to find myself again. When Erwin left, we both felt very sad, but we promised to keep in touch and were both determined to see each other again.

Unfortunately for me, my position as Sammy's nanny did not last long. His father found a job with a band in a resort hotel on the east coast. He felt they would be safer in the countryside where the bombing was less intense. I could only hope that Sammy's mother would be able to pull herself together. Sammy's father was the healthier of the two emotionally, but he too was sensitive and high-strung. I was sorry to see them go. This was the first time since leaving Vienna that I had felt wanted and needed and was able to give something of myself to help heal a human being.

BLITZ

The London Blitz began on September 7, 1940. Hitler intended to bomb the British people into submission by attacking them unrelentingly day and night. When people went out, they never knew whether their home would be standing when they returned. But the British did not give in. Their courage and patience were admirable, and their sense of humor helped them handle their anxiety and the possibility of imminent death. There was a popular joke making the rounds at the time which never failed to get a laugh.

> A couple went out to the cinema one night leaving the husband's elderly father at home. When the couple returned, their house had been bombed and all that was left was a heap of rubble. They searched frantically through the devastation to see what had become of the old man. They found him sitting on the toilet. When he saw them, he said, "All I did was pull the chain and the house fell down!"

In spite of the widespread destruction, people did not panic and there was no looting of any kind. The cooperation and helpfulness of everyone was astounding. People bombed out of their homes could seek shelter in their local community house, church, or air raid shelter. There were soup kitchens everywhere, so no one went without food. Social classes were less important than before. The philosophy of the day was "Live life to the fullest because there might be no tomorrow." For most people, this meant continuing their daily activities. Life had to go on regardless.

When the war broke out, many families left London, and thousands of children were evacuated to the country without their parents. Most of the children were placed in foster homes or hostels, and some were sent to Canada. During the Blitz thousands who stayed behind slept on the platforms of tube stations. They brought blankets, pillows, and ground sheets from home, and some even brought army cots. They got up in the morning and went to work and sent the children off to school. To me it was a sad sight, and on no occasion did I feel the need to sleep there. Sanitary conditions were not the best, although volunteer groups did make an effort to improve them. Nor was the underground as safe as people had hoped. On a few occasions high explosive bombs managed to kill people taking refuge there.

During the Blitz, warning sirens sounded several times every day and night, and bombs dropped all over the place. There were the regular bombs, which came in various weights and sizes, and there were the incendiary bombs, intended to burn down the city. There were the time bombs that caused great anxiety because no one knew when they would explode. The teams that defused these bombs were outstanding technicians, with nerves of steel. During one period, the bombers circled around and around without dropping any bombs just to torment us, which was nerve-racking. The feeling of the people was "Drop the bomb already and move on!" This technique was designed to have this very effect. Towards the end of the war the Germans devised a much more lethal bomb called the buzz bomb. These bombs, jet propelled and winged, flew horizontally, like airplanes, and the projectile was so fast that it was impossible to send out a warning signal such as a siren. These bombs could wipe out several houses simultaneously.

Three times during the Blitz I came very close to dying. One evening I was having dinner with friends whose flat was on the top floor. They had recently rearranged the furniture in their dining room, moving the table from the center of the room to one side. While we were eating, a bomb fell on the house and caved in the roof. If the table had been in its former location, we might all have been killed by falling debris.

On a second occasion, the same night I lost my dowry, my date and I were making our way through streets where incendiary bombs had set fires raging. Suddenly we heard a rush that sounded like a train coming towards us. We dashed to a four-foot wall nearby and pressed ourselves against it. Incendiary bombs rained down as we cowered against the wall. Had we been on the opposite side of the wall, both of us would have been killed.

The third incident happened when I lived in a rented room on the top floor of a boarding house. The roof had caught fire from falling shrapnel from British anti-aircraft guns. Since the only exit to the roof was through my room, the fire brigade had to climb through my window to put out the fire. I was sleeping soundly and did not learn about the incident until the next morning. I felt that a guardian angel had been watching over me.

By May 11, 1941, the Blitz had ended. Although bombs continued to fall on London, there were no longer hundreds of planes attacking every day and night. Hitler needed most of his bombers and fighter planes for his next project—the invasion of the Soviet Union.

FLOWER MAKER

By the time my employment as Sammy's nanny ended, the British government had dropped the requirement that aliens had to live where they worked. This was my opportunity to live on my own. Aliens were not allowed to do war work and it was difficult for aliens to find a decent job. I did manage to obtain a job in a factory making artificial flowers, which were in great demand in those days. We also cut and pasted fancy feathers for men's and women's hats. Of the thirty or so workers, I was the only one willing to work the powerful feather-cutting machine which had been known to cut off workers' fingers. We earned a small base salary with a supplement based on the number of flowers and bouquets we completed. The total was hardly enough to live on. Even so, I went ahead and rented a room on the top floor of a seedy boarding house in Bloomsbury.

I was elated. I had won my freedom. I was my own master, with my own space. I could make my own decisions. These feelings were so potent within me that I remember them all very clearly to this date. That I sometimes had to go without food did not overshadow my positive feelings. To earn a little more money, I brought flowers home to make bouquets. The landlady, who was a cheapskate, turned off all the lights at ten o'clock, so I worked in front of the gas heater which gave off a limited amount of light. Work left no time for social life and I hardly knew the other boarders other than to say *hello*.

Through an advertisement I finally found a single woman, a secretary, who wanted to rent part of her apartment for less than I was paying for my rather dingy room. She lived in a modern apartment building and rented me sleeping space on the couch in her dining room. The flat was nicely furnished, and I cherished the use of her well-maintained bathroom. She was not prejudiced against foreigners, a great relief for me, and we formed a good relationship.

One day while I was living there, the doorbell rang and a detective asked to come inside. Although he appeared to be friendly, he asked a lot of questions without revealing the reason for his call. He returned again and again at all hours and formed a relationship with my landlady, who finally asked him outright the reason for his visits. He told her, in confidence, that I had been seen in the company of a spy—a saboteur—and was therefore under suspicion. Out of fear, she told me what the detective had said. I was stunned and racked my brains trying to figure out who in my small circle of friends seemed suspicious. No one. I finally visited the local police station to show them my address book. I informed them that I was not a spy and had nothing to hide. They told me that they had already arrested the spy, a German refugee who had lived next to me in the boarding house in Bloomsbury. I barely knew this woman and had spoken to her only once. One day shortly after I had moved out, she spotted me on the street and kindly informed me that I had mail sitting in the hallway which the landlady had not bothered to forward. That the police no longer suspected me took a great load off my anxious mind.

The flower-making job had some drawbacks, apart from the low salary. The factory was in a commercial neighborhood where the bombing was especially intense. Another problem was my fellow workers. They resented me because I had good manual dexterity and worked much faster than they did. Whenever I took my eyes off my work for a few moments, someone would reach over and snatch some of my flowers. If I accused one of the girls, it accomplished nothing. She would just look innocent and deny it. This was the first time I experienced any kind of dishonesty in Great Britain.

While I was working in the flower factory, an advertisement in the newspaper arrested my attention. The Ballet Russe de Monte Carlo was coming to town and they needed more dancers. I had kept up my dancing as well as I could through the Austrian cultural center where I had danced solo in a few productions, so it was with high hopes that I attended the tryouts for the Ballet Russe. All went well until I was asked to turn five times on one toe. I couldn't do it. They dismissed me very politely, explaining that two weeks was not enough time to get my dancing up to the required standard. For several days after the tryouts I could barely walk. Instead of dancing with the ballet, I watched all their performances as a member of the audience.

FLOWER SELLER

It was time to move on, and I found a more suitable job. Instead of making artificial flowers I was selling fresh flowers in the flower shop at Lyons Corner House in Marble Arch in the West End. Lyons Corner House is a franchised group of tearooms that also serve short order food. It is a popular establishment in London, usually found in busy shopping centers. Before entering the restaurant, one passes through a candy store and a flower shop which frequently cater to single people meeting their dates there.

Working conditions were good. The head of the organization treated her employees well, renting a gym and hiring an instructor to conduct exercise sessions for us. We took full advantage of this opportunity, since our jobs required us to be on our feet all day. Employees were issued an attractive uniform for a small charge. Those of us in the flower and candy shops wore well-designed green dresses that made us stand out from the other employees.

Marble Arch is a very desirable neighborhood, located at the northeast corner of Hyde Park, near a fashionable hotel. Here on Sundays anyone who wanted to could stand on an orange crate and pontificate on religion or economics or philosophy or even politics. A large and diverse group gathered to listen to the speakers. There were foreigners, students, upper class English citizens, and people just out for a stroll, most of whom would drop in for a bite to eat at Lyons Corner House. Policemen would stand by to keep a watchful eye on the proceedings. It was like Chicago's once popular Bug House Square but on a much grander scale. Having recently emigrated from Nazi occupied Vienna, I was very much impressed by the freedom of speech that I witnessed at Hyde Park Corner.

ON BECOMING A LANDLADY

While working at Lyons Corner House, I met many interesting people including the Italian headwaiter who worked at the hotel next door. One day he asked me if I would be willing to rent a mews house from him. He had recently obtained a divorce from his wife and wanted to rent the furnished house where they had lived. I informed him that I could not afford to rent the place by myself but would still like to take a look at it.

The house was in Knightsbridge just opposite Harrods Department Store. At that time mews houses were very fashionable. Originally built as stables, they became garages with living quarters for the chauffeur on the second floor. Most of the garages were remodeled into charming modern homes by converting the downstairs into living and dining rooms and the upstairs into bedrooms and bathrooms. The headwaiter's house had not been converted. The living space, reached by a wrought iron staircase on the outside of the building, was exclusively upstairs. There were two sparsely furnished bedrooms, a hall, and one large kitchen which could serve as a family room, with a large box that looked like a piece of furniture hiding the stove. There was a pantry with a sink for washing dishes, and there was a storage room with a refrigerator, a bathroom, and a toilet. As simply and sparsely furnished as this place was, to me it seemed like heaven. The headwaiter found some tenants for me, and at last I had a house I could call my own, even if it was rented.

The tenants, whom I thoroughly interviewed, were attractive young Scottish girls—identical twins from Glasgow who hoped to find their fame and fortune in London. The girls were charming, innocent, enthusiastic, and willing to abide by my conditions, which were quite reasonable. Both of them worked nearby at a food specialty store.

I departed from my landlady with her best wishes and eagerly moved into my new abode. The twins followed soon after. It was interesting to observe the psychological aspects of their relationship, since at times they behaved as if they had only one ego between them. In the morning I was unable to tell them apart, but as the day wore on, I could discern minute differences in their personality and looks. They used to send each other off to date the same boy, in order to compare notes. Although they were not well educated, they were full of energy, mischief, hopes, and laughter, and I enjoyed having them as tenants. To me they represented fresh air and a new start in life. I was a landlady and in control of my destiny—at least in part.

Soon the twins started to date brothers who were also identical twins. Both worked as managers in a department store in the West End and were nice, genuine boys, as far as I could tell. After dating them for quite some time, the girl twins became engaged to the boy twins and moved to another location. We parted on good terms. The girls took their fiancés home to

Glasgow to introduce them to their family. They called me to inform me that their parents approved of their choice and that they were happy. They thanked me for helping them to become adjusted in London and for standing by them. My educated guess was that because of their pending marriages and their need to relocate, find apartments, and start a new life, they had to make great adjustments and were pushed somewhat towards maturing. However, they were unable to separate and in turn were seeking partners who displayed the same inability to function as individuals on their own.

NURSERY SCHOOL TEACHER

By looking through the advertisements in the paper, I finally found a job well suited to my abilities and interests. The ad was posted by the London County Council, an organization that supervised public nursery schools, mostly in working class areas. My interview went well, resulting in a position as nursery school teacher in Battersea, a working class district. No doubt the nursery school course I took in Vienna helped me to obtain this position.

I was impressed by the high standards of these schools. There was one teacher for every five children, and there were afternoon naps, required by the Board of Education. Also required was the administration of cod-liver oil in syrup, dipped onto a stick and generally enjoyed by most of the children. There were dance lessons and rhythmical movement exercises organized by visiting specialists, and the equipment provided was up-to-date and very therapeutic.

The toys and play equipment followed the Melanie Klein concept of play therapy. Melanie Klein, a famous Vienna-born psychoanalyst living in London, was the first to treat young children. She devised and developed a play therapy, contending that to small children, everything around them such as a chair or table looks very large. They therefore feel more secure, comfortable, and safe when expressing their feelings and anxieties through toys that they can easily manipulate and control. The London nursery schools were all equipped with her recommendations. There was water play and sand play, consisting of two large metal-lined drawers to use indoors. Due to frequent air raids, it was prudent for us to stay indoors even when the weather was good. Other play equipment included dollhouses and small dolls with moveable parts that the children could manipulate easily. There were several family members among the dolls, including fathers, mothers, grandparents, aunts, uncles, children, and babies. There were also larger toys, such as a child-sized kitchen and other furniture, and there were building blocks, modeling clay, and drawing materials. Singing time and story time were both very popular among the children. The meals were well planned, meeting specific dietary standards, and the food, bussed in at the appropriate times, was excellent. Some of these nursery schools were located in community centers which provided educational and socializing opportunities for the mothers.

The nursery school was a safe haven for the children. They were able to play, learn, and socialize at their own pace in spite of the bombs that were dropping all around them. We had access to an air raid shelter, but we rarely used it. Life had to go on, bombs or no bombs, and the calmness of the staff when the siren sounded had a calming effect on the children. Needless to say, everyone on the staff was listening to the sirens and bombs with a third ear.

Among the children, who were between three and five years old, there was little pathology, except for a few biters who were encouraged by staff members to express their anger in age-appropriate ways. There was no enuresis (bed wetting) and no other regressive symptomatology. The children were appealing, delightful, easy to work with, and receptive to our teachings, partly because, unlike many of the older children, they had not been separated from their parents.

For me, this gratifying job had only one drawback—scheduling. The school was open from seven in the morning until seven at night to accommodate the many mothers who were engaged in war work. Most of the children did not have to stay at school for the entire twelve hours, but we teachers were required to work in shifts that alternated every two weeks. No sooner did I settle in to an early-to-bed early-to-rise routine than it was time to switch to just the opposite.

CZECH GOVERNMENT IN EXILE

Working at the nursery school and living on my own gave me time to socialize. I started to get involved in some cultural activities, which I had greatly missed. As I looked around, I found that the Czech government in exile had acquired a large house which they turned into a cultural center. They offered many activities such as dances and concerts, along with classes and lectures on a multitude of subjects including literature, philosophy, and history. I enrolled in a Czech language class. Audiences at the lectures and concerts were made up of intelligent people of all ages, not all of them Czech citizens. There were British citizens, people who had fled from the Nazis, and army officers and consular people from a variety of nations. While attending activities at the center, I became acquainted with a number of interesting people, especially the consular representatives, whom I found to be friendly, sociable, and down-to-earth.

Through my friends at the center I learned that the Czech government was sponsoring a course for allied nationals given by the London School of Economics and organized by Eileen Younghusband, OBE (Order of the British Empire), who was the head of the Social Service Department at the university and was endorsed and endowed by the British Council and the Quaker Organization. The purpose of the program was to educate allied nationals to rehabilitate their fellow citizens after the war and help them return safely to their respective countries.

I was admitted to this course on a scholarship. This meant that the Czech Ministry of Health and Welfare was sponsoring me not only to attend the courses but also to receive a small stipend for my living expenses. In return, I signed a contract promising to work for one year wherever the Czech government thought I could be most helpful. I was thrilled to be given this opportunity to learn and be trained in a helping profession.

RENATE

The time of the twins' departure from the mews house proved opportune. My friend Renate, who had been like a sister to me back in Vienna, was now living in England, and she and her baby Ruth needed a place to stay. Renate and her boyfriend Max had emigrated to London where they married and had a baby. Max had joined the British Army as a private and was sent abroad, and Renate was awaiting his return.

I had recently received a short letter from Mother saying that she had to go on a trip. She never wrote to me again. Intuitively and also obviously I knew that she had been deported and that this was the end, although it was not until the late 1950s that I learned the details of her fate.

With distress and concern for Mother constantly on my mind, I found it reassuring to have Renate, a friend from home, sharing the house with me. However, Renate had changed. Her parents and her aunt had been deported and had died in a concentration camp. She had lost her chance at a law degree when Nazi students beat her up and threw her out of the university. Even if she had completed her law degree, she could not have used it in England because she was trained in Roman law, not common law. Renate never found work in England, and it was sad to see her not trying to find an occupation suitable to her aptitude and general knowledge. Not surprisingly she focused exclusively on her family. Her grim experiences had affected her personality, which was the case for many of the Jewish people who had suffered severe degradations and losses.

Although Renate and I were close friends, living together was not easy. She was slow in her general movements and slow in completing a task. She was also messy, and it seemed that meeting her baby's wants and needs was an all-day proposition that took over the entire house. Ruth was a chubby, lovable little girl, but after a whole day of tending to the children at the nursery school, I was emotionally drained and needed some quiet time and a place to rest. I also needed a place where I could study and contemplate, because I was about to start the course at the London School of Economics. Renate and I were still close friends, but since she expected Max to return soon from the army, I decided to rent an apartment of my own and leave the mews house to Renate and her family. She supported my decision and looked forward to having the mews house to herself.

CHELSEA

With little money at my disposal, I started to look for an apartment. To me, Chelsea seemed the right district, an area thought to be arty, *avant guard,* and tolerant of free thinkers and people who were not always in step with the straight-laced general society. Many artists lived in Chelsea, including the famous Welsh Post-Impressionist, Augustus John.

After some exploration I found what seemed the right abode, the top two floors of a three-story house near Kingsrow, a main street lined with antique stores, art stores, galleries, and exhibits of Asian art. Two lesbian nurses occupied the first floor apartment. One flight up the stairs was a door which opened to my kitchen, which contained an adequate stove and oven, a sink, a refrigerator, and a large bathtub covered by a removable wooden plank which served as a kitchen table. The toilet, on the same floor, was separate. On the top floor there were two rooms, one of them quite large and bright, with two big windows overlooking the street. This room looked as if it might have been an artist's studio, but I could use it as a combination living room, bedroom, dining room, and study. The other room was smaller and darker but could serve as a storage room. The top two floors had been partially destroyed by bombs, and the repair work was plainly visible from both the inside and the outside of the building.

In spite of the unusual layout, I liked the apartment very much. The rent was low, I would have a quiet work space, and in the small backyard, there was an air raid shelter, which satisfied my angst. My rationalization was that a building once bombed is unlikely to be bombed again. Without hesitation I eagerly rented the apartment. I acquired an easy chair, four folding chairs, a bridge table, and a couch to sit on and sleep on, and I improvised a dressing table by making a chintz skirt for a leather trunk which my mother had sent to me full of elegant clothes. I found an inexpensive but beautiful antique writing desk and prepared to become a student once again.

Chapter Five

Back to School

As much as I hated leaving my job at the nursery school, it felt really good—like the right thing to do—to be continuing my interrupted education. I found my studies in the Social Welfare program at the London School of Economics to be highly stimulating. There were courses in psychology, physiology, early childhood development, the juvenile court of Britain, administration, social welfare, anatomy, and contagious diseases. The teachers were excellent, and the students, twenty-five in all, were a highly motivated group of public servants.

Of all the psychoanalysts I was exposed to during my time at the London School of Economics, I was most impressed by Melanie Klein, who taught the course in early childhood development and whose concept of play therapy was used by the public nursery schools in London, including the one in Battersea where I had taught. Because of her ability to be in touch with her inner young child, Klein was very much aware of youngsters' nonverbal communications and believed that an analyst can gain insights into young children's unconscious by observing them as they play. Although her theoretical framework was different and innovative, Klein was not always given the credit she deserved in psychoanalytic circles. She was the originator of the object-relations theory which stresses the importance of the interaction between the infant and the mothering person, the results of which have a lasting effect on the developmental growth process of a child. Although the object-relations theory has been practiced in Great Britain and South America for many years, it was slow to gain acceptance in the United States. The Center for Psychoanalytic Study in Chicago was one of the first institutions in the United States to implement Melanie Klein's theoretical framework.

I found Melanie Klein to be alert, non-assuming, and highly intelligent, a person who radiated inner peace. Although she had to endure great hardships in her life, her dignity and ego-strength helped her get through difficult times. My whole orientation as a psychoanalyst was significantly influenced by Klein's teaching, conceptual framework, and stoic personality.

As part of our training at the London School of Economics, we had to pass an examination that qualified us to become an official Red Cross worker, able to bandage broken limbs, fashion a splint, apply a tourniquet, and resuscitate a person. To be able to accomplish all this with understanding, we were given courses in biology and first aid. We met at each other's homes to practice first aid, timing ourselves as we did so. At the home of Lady Fletcher, a white Russian who had married an English Lord, I met and became good friends with a lieutenant in the Belgian army. She told me that she had been parachuted into Belgium in order to sabotage German invaders. At times she was unable to attend class because her military duties did not allow it. I admired her greatly for her fortitude and guts.

The other unusual task we were assigned involved military-type training by the British Council for Rehabilitation which included camping outdoors. We were assigned to a field near Oxford for a ten-day training session. Our instructor showed us how to pitch a bell tent, dig a latrine, collect firewood, and cook over an open fire. We learned to create a slow, smoldering fire suitable for heating water for tea by filling a gasoline drum with damp sawdust, pushing a broom handle into the center to aerate the sawdust, and then igniting the sawdust. We slept on ground sheets in sleeping bags and showered in a bathhouse nearby, making do with as little equipment as possible. We were separated into teams and competed with each other to see who could gather the most firewood from the forest and cook the best meals. We grew close to each other and enjoyed the experience except for the cold rainy weather and the cows that occasionally came into our tents at night and licked our toes. At the end of the ten days when we returned to civilization, I had trouble sleeping in a closed room, nor could I sleep in a bed for quite some time.

While stationed in Germany, I never had to camp out. Nevertheless, I was glad to have had this experience. It gave me new appreciation of things we take for granted like having a stove to cook on. Most of all, I appreciated what we learned about team spirit, which I developed and used to good advantage while working for UNRRA. Although there were Dutch, Norwegian, Swedish, French, and Czech nationals in our group, each with our own cultural background and customs and beliefs, we got on very well. The English language, the atmosphere, and the courses we took united us all, and our aim was the same—to help those desolate persons pick themselves up and return to their homeland unharmed.

During my time at the London School of Economics I formed three lasting friendships—two with Czech nationals and one with Kit Stewart, the assistant to Miss Younghusband. Kit was warm, giving, inspiring, and supportive of all the students. She took a special interest in me and had a great influence on my professional growth. She also provided me with a once-in-a-lifetime social occasion. One day she took another student and me to Buckingham Palace where she introduced us to the ladies in waiting to the Queen.

Without being entirely conscious of it, I had gradually become acculturated to English ways. This was precipitated by my living on my own and making British friends who were supportive, steadfast, and sincere. By living in this society I had adopted its mannerisms, general behavior, and thinking processes. I had a strong need to belong somewhere and no longer felt like an outsider. My German accent was less pronounced and I had become proficient in the English language. The courses I took at the London School of Economics broadened my horizons. I felt comfortable enough with English to ask many questions in class and to read a wide variety of books in English, including many books on child development, especially books by Susan Isaacs. Isaacs, who was one of Melanie Klein's object-relations oriented psychoanalysts, had a great influence on me.

TAVISTOCK CLINIC

When my initial training came to an end, the Czech Ministry of Social Welfare chose five students, including me, to be trained to work with emotionally disturbed children. The program was designed and executed by the Tavistock Clinic, a training center for psychoanalysts. The course, headed by Dr. Singer, a Czech psychoanalyst trained by the clinic, consisted of field placements into institutions for emotionally disturbed children.

Before this course was organized and underway, the Czech Ministry of Social Welfare sent me to their residential nursery school, a sizable estate near Northampton which harbored seventy Czech children and infants and one hundred Czech adults. Most of the adults were mothers employed by the institution. I arrived wearing a Red Cross uniform and was immediately put in charge of a room full of infants suffering from whooping cough. Doctors and nurses were in residence and I took great care of the infants, but I was working under the watchful eyes of their mothers, all of whom made sure that their baby was not shortchanged. All the adults gave their rationing books to the head cook so that the children would be assured of a well-balanced diet. Food rationing was grim. We were served dandelions and thistles which grew in abundance on the estate and tasted like spinach.

One of my assignments was teaching nursery school children. Another task, assigned to all employees, was to do one week of night duty every two weeks. Night duty involved changing the diapers of all the infants of whom there were quite a few. Once again I found it difficult to change schedules from week to week.

Perhaps because there were so many people occupying the estate, there was not enough heat. After finishing our work with the children, we had to chop wood to feed the potbelly stove in the employees' room. This presented quite a hardship for all of us.

ALLENDALE

For the course on emotionally disturbed children, two of us were sent to Allendale School in Aylesbury, about forty miles northwest of London. Dr. Singer was to visit us every week and lecture us, at the same time evaluating our performance. Allendale was an Approved School, an institution administered by the juvenile court for girls who had been convicted of a misdemeanor and had to remain there for three years. More severe offenders were incarcerated in the Borstal. The court system in Great Britain is known for its benign and humanitarian approach towards delinquent youths, with a strong emphasis on rehabilitation. When the United States, specifically Chicago, made an attempt to follow Great Britain's example, the effort unfortunately phased out after a short lifecycle.

Allendale School stood behind an iron fence that announced its name at the top of the front gate. To me, it seemed like a regular school except for its locked doors and the somewhat rigid rules and regulations, which were needed to give both internal and external structure to the lives of these children. The girls wore a uniform consisting of a dark blue skirt or jumper, a white blouse, a navy blue coat, and a hat with a rounded brim. The words "Allendale School" were sewn onto the top of their sleeves. The place was well staffed and the children were treated well, as far as we could observe. The youngsters, whose ages ranged from ten to fifteen, lived in dormitories supervised by a warden who saw that they kept their rooms in order and that hygienic standards were observed.

One of my assignments was to take a young-looking eleven-year-old girl to a clinic every week to receive treatment for syphilis. Every time we went there, a staff member mistook me for the patient and the child for my daughter. The child remained silent most of the time, and any effort on my part to start a conversation was without avail. Perhaps she was ashamed and embarrassed. A resident probation officer took the two of us under her wing and so did a resident psychologist.

My main assignment was to act as teacher to twenty-five of the older children, an unruly lot who were quite rambunctious in the classroom. Getting their attention was not an easy task. At first they hardly allowed me to speak, drowning me out with screams, shouts, and verbal attacks. Their mouthing off in this way indicated to me that I was a threat to them. I decided to broaden their information about the war. I began by asking them what they already knew and by showing interest in their responses. They liked my approach and especially liked the fact that I listened to them with interest. Gradually the girls calmed down and listened as I told them of my first-hand experiences with the Nazis in occupied Vienna and what I had to go through before fleeing to England. They started to identify with me and began to turn into a receptive and active student body.

While teaching this group, I became acquainted with some of the girls. There was Betty, who looked and acted like a waif, and Josie, who was particularly needy and downtrodden. I suspected that many of these youngsters came from emotionally and economically deprived backgrounds and were in need of personal attention and care. There was a great deal of free-floating hostility and anger amongst many of these girls, but I could see that the structured and stable environment had a calming effect. Most of them eventually learned to exercise some self-control.

Since my colleague and I were the first foreign students to be placed in the institution, the administration did not quite know how to handle us. We were not allowed to attend the group meetings with the youngsters and the psychologist. It seemed to us that the school was overly cautious and guarded in the way they tried to keep us from learning more about the inner workings of the institution. They never let us know what offenses the youngsters had committed, information we could have used to good advantage.

ANNA FREUD AND HER BARN

Anna Freud, the daughter of Sigmund Freud, had two vacancies for live-in residents-in-training at The Barn, a farm house in Essex converted into a treatment center for emotionally disturbed children. Anna Freud ran this center together with her partner and associate Dorothy Burlingham. She approached Dr. Singer, who eagerly agreed to let her pick two students from our group. She interviewed each of us in her father's house in Hampstead. I was impressed by the large number of books in the house. Even the staircase was lined with bookcases. I felt happy and honored to be chosen as one of two students to attend The Barn as a resident. The other student, a Czech woman who had a law degree from the University of Prague, was to work with the older children while I was to be with the younger children. The Barn was located in Essex, far away from any town, and it took nearly a whole day of changing trains for us to get there.

There were about sixty children and one hundred adults residing at The Barn. Most of the children came from bombed out homes, and their families, for a variety of reasons, were unable to care for them. Anna Freud and Dorothy Burlingham handled the intake of the children, whose ages ranged from five to fourteen. Parents and other relatives could visit the children on weekends. Some of the visits were supervised by the staff, depending on the diagnostic evaluation of the family situation.

When my colleague and I first arrived at The Barn, we were eager to start working with the children but instead were assigned to kitchen duty (shades of the past). Anna Freud was concerned that the children would feel threatened if exposed to strangers. She wanted them to get used to us gradually while watching us work in the kitchen. Our kitchen duty lasted for two long weeks, during which some of the children exchanged a few words with us or asked us to help them tie their shoes.

At the end of the two week period I was asked to accompany the younger children and their teacher on a walk in the vast meadows near their home. During the walk I bent down to smell a flower. The children descended on me like a mob, knocking me down, beating me up, and pulling my hair, which was long and fixed in a bun on the top of my head.

Their behavior took me completely by surprise. I felt shocked and helpless, and sitting on the ground, I started to cry. The children ran away home, probably feeling guilty for their behavior. Their teacher was nowhere to be seen. Anna Freud had been right about the children feeling threatened by newcomers, but two weeks was not long enough for them to feel safe with us, especially since we had not been adequately introduced to them by the adults. The children's actions revealed their high levels of pent-up anxiety, anger, and rage. Whatever their experiences had been, they certainly felt very insecure, vulnerable, and separated from their protected environment, in this case The Barn, or they would not have lashed out at me.

The residential staff at The Barn consisted primarily of German-speaking immigrants. The students, of whom there were quite a few, came from all over Europe, including France, Belgium, Holland, and Norway. Anna Freud received financial support for The Barn from America and other European countries but nothing from the British government because of her decision not to follow the rules and regulations set up by the Board of Education. Unlike the children at the public nursery schools, the children at The Barn did not receive a daily dose of cod liver oil nor did the younger children take afternoon naps. Anna Freud did not believe that her children needed naps. Instead they were taken on escorted walks in the countryside. I found the children to be tired and cranky after lunch, and by bedtime they were usually over-stimulated and had a hard time going to sleep. This was the time of day when their defenses were low and they missed their loved ones most. We spent a lot of time with each child at bedtime and helped them with their anxieties, longings, and feelings of separation and abandonment. This seemed to make a great difference to them emotionally.

Anna Freud had an impressive appearance. She never followed any kind of fashion but instead wore dresses resembling an Austrian dirndl. When fashion dictated short skirts, her skirts remained long. Her long grayish brown hair was gathered in a bun at the back of her neck. She was always soft spoken and displayed a charming and endearing personality, underlying which seemed to be a great deal of self-assurance, at times even arrogance. No matter what people's previous experience had been, she made them feel that they knew nothing until they came under her tutelage. To some degree this was true. What she taught us was new and fresh, a theoretical framework known to no one else with the exception of her father. Encouraged by her father, she conceptualized the treatment of children. But she did things her own way and never agreed with the brilliant conceptual framework of Melanie Klein, who was the first to analyze very young children with great success.

Although Anna Freud spent most of her time at her clinic in London, she made regular weekly visits to The Barn. During these visits she lectured us and clinically evaluated the functioning and behavior of each child as presented by the staff. Her input was astute and to the point, especially her diagnostic evaluation and recommendation on how to treat each individual child. This process provided a great learning experience for all of us and we valued it highly.

Anna Freud, who had been trained as an elementary school teacher in Vienna, had definite ideas on the raising of children. One of her beliefs was that young children should not have to say *please* and *thank you*, since they do not have the sophistication to understand why this is important. One of the first words most English babies are taught to say is *ta*, which means *thank you*. Before a child is given a gift or a piece of cake, for example, the parent or caretaker asks "What do you say?" and the child is expected to answer "Ta." The parent or caretaker, in Anna Freud's view, is demanding this behavior not as a valid part of the child's learning experience but as a means of control. Another of Anna Freud's strong opinions was that parents exert too much control over what their children eat. She felt that, within limits, children should be allowed to eat what they liked. The staff took this interpretation literally. During mealtimes we observed that one child ate only potatoes while others ate only gravy and others ate only meat. I suggested that the adults should sit and eat with the children, thereby redirecting their food fads toward more nutritious habits. The director of the institution, Alice Goldberger, put my suggestion into practice. This had a calming effect on the children. There was far less acting out behavior, such as throwing food around, and the children began to eat a more balanced diet.

We had two nonresident professionals at The Barn—a dance teacher and an occupational therapist. The dance teacher arrived in the evening, and all the children and some of the adults participated in and greatly enjoyed English country dancing. The occupational therapist supervised the garden. The children were each given a small patch of land, about six feet by four feet, and allowed to plant whatever they wished. Some children grew potatoes and onions while others planted tomatoes and beans, usually coupled with annuals like daisies and geraniums. They loved to dig in the dirt and eat their harvested vegetables. The whole project was very therapeutic for the children.

I thoroughly enjoyed my stay at The Barn—the stimulating program, the professionals and students I met, the children, and most of all, Anna Freud and what she gave to all of us in terms of therapeutic knowledge and know-how relating to her newly developed theoretical framework about childhood growth and development and the treatment of the individual child.

ANNA FREUD AND MELANIE KLEIN CONTROVERSY

In 1926 Austrian-born Melanie Klein was invited by the British psychoanalyst Ernest Jones, founder and president of the British Psychoanalytical Society, to come to London to lecture and practice. She was enthusiastically received in England and was well established there. In 1938, when Anna Freud fled from Vienna to London with her father, she demanded that her theories be heard. Although Melanie Klein admired Sigmund Freud and was close to him, she found herself in direct conflict with his daughter. The ensuing debates rocked the foundations of the British Psychoanalytical Society. The following summary, based on a paper I gave on the subject, highlights their major points of disagreement.

When Analysis Should be Undertaken

Anna Freud believed that no child under the age of six could benefit from psychoanalysis and that "the analysis of a child is opportune only when real infantile neurosis is actually present."[1] She also felt that children should not be analyzed unless one of their parents was a psychoanalyst or had been analyzed. Melanie Klein, on the other hand, believed that even very young children could benefit from psychoanalysis and stated that every disturbance of the psychic or intellectual development of the child can be removed or at least be favorably influenced by analysis.[2]

The Beginning Formation of the Superego

Freud believed that the superego of the child develops after the oedipal period has been concluded, while Klein believed that the Superego was present in very young children and that it was a primitive and savage one which dealt with primary process material which she obtained from her analysis of her young patients (for example, the wish to eat up the mother's breast).

Transference Relationship

"Transference" is the transferring over to the therapist the feelings a child has towards his parents, mainly in fantasy. Freud's contention was that young children are too attached to their parents to be able to form a transference relationship with the analyst. She believed that if such a transference within the treatment occurred, it needed to be eliminated. Klein was of the opinion that children do form a transference relationship with their therapist which becomes a very important diagnostic and treatment tool. She felt that the expression of negative feelings in the treatment situation liberates the ego, is very helpful in furthering a positive relationship, and has a curative effect, releasing guilt feelings and anxiety.

Attitude of Children toward Their Analysis

Anna Freud contended that children should be brought to a realization of their illness or "naughtiness" and to a definite wish for a cure. Melanie Klein, on the other hand, thought this to be quite superfluous.

The Role of the Unconscious in the Analysis of Children

Anna Freud stated that "in the output of material from the unconscious, child analysis stands far behind adult analysis" and it "does not lead us beyond the boundaries where the child becomes capable of speech."[3] Klein thought that young children can easily understand conscious and unconscious interpretations because they have developed fewer defenses and therefore are in touch with their primitive feelings and desires.

These discussions helped Melanie Klein to focus and further refine her psychoanalytic concepts. She believed that free play in children is equivalent to free association in adults.

After this intense debate, which lasted from January 1943 to May 1944, the British Psychoanalytical Society broke into three factions. One group followed Melanie Klein's conceptual framework, one group followed Anna Freud's, and a third group took some concepts from both. One member of this "Middle Group" was Dr. Donald W. Winnicott, an English pediatrician who understood young children very well and went on to become a creative child psychoanalyst developing his own conceptual framework for the understanding, diagnosis, and treatment of children from infancy on. In Great Britain these three groups exist to the present day. I have learned a great deal from all three psychoanalysts and admire their work.

Time moved too quickly. I had to leave The Barn because the Czech government assigned me to serve with UNRRA—The United Nations Relief and

Rehabilitation Administration. I left early in the morning of VE Day, with Germany as the ultimate destination.[4]

NOTES

1. Anna Freud, "Short History of Child Analysis," *The Psychoanalytic Study of Child* (New Haven, CT, 1966), 21, 7-14.

2. Hanna Segal, *Klein* (London, Karnac Books and The Institute of Psycho-Analysis, 1989), 91-112.

3. Segal, 91-112.

4. The reader may be interested to note that after the war Dr. Singer became the head of Mental Health and Welfare in Czechoslovakia, and my Czech colleague at The Barn became the Attorney General of Czechoslovakia.

Chapter Six

Germany

UNRRA

On November 9, 1943, representatives of forty-four nations gathered at the White House in Washington DC and signed a document establishing the first international relief agency in world history—The United Nations Relief and Rehabilitation Administration. This was an affirmative acknowledgment to those desolate persons behind German and Japanese lines that they had not been forgotten. From 1945 to 1947 UNRRA operated in seventeen war-torn countries. Their slogan was "UNRRA helps those who can help themselves." UNRRA locomotives moved transportation that had come to a standstill. UNRRA tractors helped to harvest once barren fields. Food distribution through UNRRA eliminated famine in war-torn countries, and medical supplies through UNRRA prevented epidemics. All these initiatives can be categorized as relief. Without them, Europe would not have been able to get back on its feet in such a short period of time. UNRRA gave the world breathing space in the struggle for recovery, preventing widespread starvation, curbing epidemics, and averting economic collapse.

Most important in my opinion was something else UNRRA did. It was the first international agency to go out into the world and wrestle with the problems that come with peace. It was a global approach to a global problem. Never before had an international group of civil servants worked side by side for one cause, in this case, to help the war-torn countries and displaced persons to return to a more normal way of life.

The staff of UNRRA was multinational and multilingual. A large number of these civil servants were placed in the displaced persons camps and assembly centers in Germany, Austria, Italy, the Middle East, and China. There were forty nations represented on the staff, a great body of international civil servants. Many of these were experts in the fields of administration, procurement, agriculture, transportation, engineering, social welfare, public health, medicine, finance, accounting, communications, and aerial transportation. UNRRA, whose budget totaled $3.7 billion, was funded by its member governments. Each member government that had not been occupied by the Nazis was asked to contribute two percent of its annual income for relief supplies and services, and all invaded countries were asked to contribute what they could.

After the war it was estimated that there were eight million displaced persons in Germany alone, most of them Nazi labor slaves and concentration camp inhabitants. The majority of the persons on forced labor wanted to go home but had no means of getting there. Some did not wish to return because they were political refugees, racial refugees, or deserters and regarded themselves as stateless. These people became the concern of UNRRA. Excluded from its concern were prisoners of war and persons who had collaborated with the enemy or committed war crimes. [1]

In addition to the adult displaced persons there were thousands of "unaccompanied children" in Europe who often knew neither their name nor their nationality. Some of them had spent their entire life in concentration camps, had seen their parents mutilated or killed, and were badly mistreated and abused themselves. Some children had been hidden by farmers and some had lived in groups in woods and caves. To give these abandoned children psychological and physical care, UNRRA established special camps. The centers for children usually had a more pleasant physical setup than the adult centers and were more fully staffed. At first there were about ten thousand children in these camps but their ranks were soon swelled by thousands who came out of hiding, were located by UNRRA search teams, or who immigrated from Eastern Europe, mostly Hungarian Jews.

Any new organization has teething problems. Unfortunately there were some UNRRA workers who took advantage of their position and made money for themselves on the black market. Most of these were singled out and duly dismissed from the agency. Not surprisingly, these bad actors received special attention in newspapers and on the radio, and this did not reflect well on UNRRA, effectively blurring the many constructive acts this agency later became known for.

VE DAY

It was VE Day—May 8, 1945. The war in Europe had finally come to an end and I was in London. My duffle bag was bulging, and what with my spare uniform, jumpsuit, heavy overcoat, all designed for British officers, first aid kit, blankets, spare shoes, and combat boots, the weight of the bag was quite considerable. The streets of London were crowded with everyone celebrating the end of war, the end of bombing, and the end of anxiety, fear, loss, and separation. People were shouting, crying, and waving flags. It was a great day for all of us. No one seemed to care that every restaurant and bar was closed. There was no food available for anyone, especially not for me, since the cupboard in my Chelsea flat was empty after my long sojourn in Essex.

I became emotional, along with everyone else. I was leaving for an unknown land and situation, first to Normandy for a special training program, then to Germany to help the displaced persons. At the back of my mind was the hope that in Germany I would find out what had happened to the rest of my family. This was one of the motivating forces that had made me eager to participate in this training in the first place. My heart trembled with joy, anticipation, and some anxiety, since I did not know what to expect.

EN ROUTE TO NORMANDY

In London the sun was shining and a warm breeze caressed our faces, but as we crossed the English Channel and arrived in Calais, the weather turned most inclement, with heavy fog everywhere. Paris was cool and cloudy.

There were just three UNRRA personnel, all of us women, coming from England—an English girl, another Czech citizen, and me. I do not know why the three of us had been selected for the special course in Normandy. Perhaps we had shown some leadership capabilities or had had some advanced training.

In Calais we waited for more than an hour for a somewhat primitive local train to arrive. We packed ourselves in like sardines among French soldiers, peasants, and a variety of refugees who were trying to get home to their loved ones. Food smells penetrated the car. Some people held long baguettes which they ate with gusto—and with cheese. Others were eating dried sausages. As for us, we had been given K-rations, canned food and stale crackers which tasted a little like sand and had to last us for three days and nights, the time it took for the train to arrive in Normandy. The comradeship amongst the passengers was remarkable in spite of the crowded conditions. The war was over. People were going home. Our small group grew close to each other, sharing our food, what little there was of it, and supporting each other in our free-floating anxiety.

Our destination in Normandy was a hotel between Granville and Jullouville, both of which are well-known summer resorts. The hotel had been inhabited by a group of German soldiers who had tried to invade Normandy from the Channel Islands right after the war and were apprehended. For their own enjoyment they had painted hideous pictures of nude women all over the walls of the restaurant and reception halls. Our group of specially selected UNRRA personnel and our instructors were the only inhabitants of this hotel.

FURTHER TRAINING

Our instructors were knowledgeable, well trained, and experienced. They came from many nationalities including British, American, French, Dutch, and Cuban. I was particularly impressed with the Cuban physician who taught us a great deal about infectious diseases and how to cope with them.

Our courses ranged from the economic and political situation in Germany to public speaking, administration, legal matters, and geographical situations such as the various zones Germany was divided into. A lot of practical information was pumped into us in a relatively short period, all of which would prove to be most useful.

During this sojourn we had time to explore our neighborhood, including the beautiful beaches and Mont Saint Michel, the medieval monastery. We moved around in groups, enjoying each other's company. Occasionally we stopped at one of the picturesque local taverns and sipped calvados, a native apple brandy so powerful that it had to be chased with beer. Although we all came from different countries, we were united in our aim—to help children, adolescents, and adults to find shelter, reunite with their families, and in the long run, develop a decent and self-respecting life in a country where they could thrive.

Among the friends I made at this time were two British gentlemen— Colonel Wattleworth, retired from the British army, and Mr. Blackburn, a stately, highly intelligent Irishman. Both men later became Area Directors for UNRRA, administering several camps for displaced persons of a variety of nationalities. Both men wanted me to join their team, and I did join Colonel Wattleworth's team several months later when I was appointed director of Camp Aschau. Other new friends were a Belgian UNRRA official and a mental health nurse from New Zealand.

When we finished our studies in Normandy, we were sent to the assembly center in Nijmegen, Holland, where a large group of UNRRA personnel were waiting to be called into the field. On the way we stopped in Brussels for a couple of days where I had my first regular restaurant meal since the rationing in London. The meal was such an event that I still remember the menu: an asparagus hors d'oeuvre, turtle soup, roast veal with cauliflower and new potatoes, and for dessert, cheese, fruit, and strawberry ice cream.

At the assembly center in Nijmegen time was lagging and morale was low. Everyone was eager to be sent out to work but assignments were not forthcoming and no one had received any mail for quite some time. We decided to send a delegation to UNRRA headquarters in the US Zone of

Germany to find out what was wrong. Tired of waiting for something to happen, I volunteered for the job, along with two older men, one British and one American. The camp administration supplied us with a weapons carrier, a contribution to UNRRA from the British government. We received some food and off we went, with everyone's blessing.

ENEMY TERRITORY

My first night in Germany was very hard on me. All my experiences with Nazis in Austria and my concern about my family in Nazi Germany were reactivated. We stopped in Bonn over night but I could not sleep. Everywhere I looked there were German men wandering the streets in their black Nazi boots. Clothes worn by the Germans were a dead giveaway of their political views. They seemed proud to be wearing this gear.

Fortunately for us our trip did not take us via the autobahn, a freeway which at that time had no speed limits. We found out later that Germans, resenting the presence of US forces, had strung invisible wires across the autobahn for the purpose of beheading GIs and officers driving fast in open jeeps. A few men were beheaded before the US Army rectified the situation by installing wire cutters near the windshield in front of the jeeps.

We arrived in Frankfurt where the headquarters of USFET (United States Forces of the European Theater) were located. The large impressive buildings of the I.G. Farben Chemical Company had been confiscated to house USFET. We stopped at a hotel managed by the American army, the only building left standing in the area. The whole city had been all but wiped out by allied bombing.

We soon ascertained why nothing was happening at the UNRRA camp near Nijmegen. The APO (Army Post Office) was serving the US Zone, the French Zone, and the British Zone only. Holland, not part of any zone, was not on their list, and no one at the APO knew there was an UNRRA camp there. We rectified the mistake and understood how it had come about. The war had only recently ended and there was bound to be some confusion. Still, the Dutch government or UNRRA should have informed the APO of the presence of this camp.

At last I was given an assignment. I was placed into the military government in Marburg in the American Zone in Germany. Replacing an American captain who was shipped home, I was given the task of caring for the displaced persons in the *Landkreis* (local land area), most of whom were Latvians, Estonians, and Lithuanians who had come to Germany of their own free will but now wanted to go home. I was to help them migrate home to their respective countries.

In spite of working in the American Zone, I was housed with a French team in the French Zone near the Swiss border. I had to brush up on my French because none of the team members wanted to speak English. Once again I was a foreign intruder.

I have no knowledge of where my two colleagues were assigned. It all happened so fast, they just sort of faded away. When I last spoke to them, they had no idea what their assignment might be.

DACHAU

Not long after we arrived in Germany, a group of UNRRA officers, myself among them, were transported to view Dachau, the first concentration camp and one of the worst. Before we arrived, we were shown hideous pictures of the camp as it looked at the time of Liberation, in late April 1945. Among them were photographs of emaciated corpses stacked like dead cattle in a sick, compulsive order with a heap of shoes on one side and a pile of rags on the other. Shortly after the Liberation, American soldiers had forced local German civilians to bury these bodies in mass graves, to make sure they understood exactly what had been going on at the camp. There was also a picture of a lamp reputed to have been made from human skin. Our group arrived long before Dachau was cleaned up for tourists, and visiting the camp was the most horrifying experience of my life. Neither the bombing of London nor my life-threatening experiences at that time compared with it. We saw large piles of dead bodies, which must have been prisoners who died after Liberation of typhus or starvation or both. Nor will I ever forget the unbearable stench. One UN representative who visited Dachau fourteen months after the Liberation could still detect the odor of burned flesh.

The entire experience left me wondering how a so-called civilized society could revert to such inhuman ways. Primitive man showed more compassion when killing animals than those twentieth century Nazis who sadistically planned these atrocities in the highly orderly and compulsive manner revealed at Dachau.

In 1938 the late Dr. Bruno Bettelheim was an inmate of Dachau. He wrote an article about his experiences there which the British military required as mandatory reading for officers sent to Germany during the war. In the article Dr. Bettelheim vividly described how all functions of the mind and body of a concentration camp inhabitant were controlled by the Nazis—all functions, that is, except for elimination. His statement, "I shit, therefore I am" was a most touching and appropriate utterance.

CAMP FOEHRENWALD

The displaced persons program was starting to take shape and after about a month in Marburg I was transferred to the first DP camp in the US Zone—Camp Foehrenwald, which means "Pine Forest," in Bavaria.

The camp, which had the capacity to house two thousand, harbored a multitude of nationalities. There were Estonians, Latvians, Lithuanians, and Polish nationals, with the largest and most needy group being the Jewish displaced persons. Most of the Jewish DPs came from Poland. Of the three million Jews who lived in Poland in 1939, about ninety per cent had been murdered by the Nazis. Most of the rest had fled to the Soviet Union during the war and returned to Poland only to be met with anti-Semitism once again. So they came to the American Zone of Germany hoping ultimately to emigrate to Palestine. The few Jews remaining in Poland tried to hide their religious beliefs but continued to be purged by the Soviet regime and the anti-Semitic Poles who took over. The second largest group at the camp were Hungarian Jews, who were persecuted near the end of the war. They came in droves, and it was heart-wrenching to hear the stories of the intense persecutions they had undergone. There were very few German Jews, very few Czechoslovakian Jews, and hardly any Austrian Jews in the DP camps. They had either been exterminated or had fled.

Communication was not too difficult. All the nationalities at the camp could speak German, the second language of educated Europeans, and all the Jewish people spoke Yiddish. Each of the nationalities mixed in a few Polish, Latvian, and Hungarian words. Since I was fluent in German and somewhat familiar with Yiddish, I was able to communicate well with all nationals and served as a translator on several occasions for Mrs. Henshaw, the Canadian director. I always felt quite sympathetic to the plight of the displaced persons. Were it not for my fleeing to England, I might have been one of them. Fortunately I was able to differentiate my feelings without being over-identified with the group. Yet my empathy was there and I am sure it showed in my work. It is interesting to note that the Latvian Jews were the best educated and most respected. The camp president, who was elected and later re-elected, was a Latvian.

Camp Foehrenwald was a showcase, visited by such dignitaries as General Eisenhower and General Patton. The camp and General Eisenhower's visit appeared prominently in the award-winning documentary film *A Long Way Home*. I make two very brief appearances in this film greeting General Eisenhower.

For its first few months the camp served as an assembly center for people of different nationalities. When General Eisenhower and General Patton visited, the camp military director, Mrs. Henshaw, and I acted as hosts and showed them around. General Eisenhower reluctantly agreed to give a speech to the camp inhabitants, and I was asked to translate his speech into German. He told me that he had never before encountered such a beautiful translator and wanted me to include that in his speech. I turned red with embarrassment, but he grew very stern and insisted that I translate his compliment, which I finally did. General Eisenhower wanted his talk to raise the morale of the several hundred people who filed into the mess hall. He reassured them that the US government was behind them and would make every effort to help them return home or to any other country. The speech was a big success. His visit and part of his speech were recorded and filmed and appeared on the evening news and in movie houses in the United States. General Eisenhower visited the camp on other occasions as well, and acting on recommendations in the Harrison Report, turned Foehrenwald into a camp exclusively for Jews, while the other DPs were transferred to camps of their own nationalities.

I found General Eisenhower to be a sincere, well-balanced, even-tempered, and courteous person who listened to other people and took note of them. He shook hands with me on several occasions and thanked me for showing him around the camp and serving as his interpreter. Although he ran a tight ship and dealt efficiently with the difficult tasks at hand, everyone liked him, soldiers and civilians alike. General Patton, on the other hand, presented himself as a rough and tough person, an uncut diamond. His soldiers were afraid of him and he did not enjoy the popularity that General Eisenhower did.

On one occasion I could not help but overhear a conversation, or rather an argument, between General Patton and General Eisenhower. I was standing far away and could not hear every word, but I could hear General Patton saying over and over again in a small voice, "But Ike, but Ike, but Ike..." while General Eisenhower sternly replied, "This is how it is and this is how it is going to be."

Camp Foehrenwald, sturdily built and well equipped, was originally a workers' camp for Germans who worked in the I.G. Farben chemical factory which was located nearby. The I.G. Farben company was well known in the United States and had a number of contracts with US chemical companies. It is interesting to note that most of the factories owned by this giant company were not bombed. Many of them were well camouflaged and had grass growing on the roof, but I sometimes wondered why so many of them were left standing. During the war the company cooperated closely with the Nazis. They held the patent for the pesticide used in the gas chambers and used slave labor to build new facilities. Directors of the company figured prominently in the Nuremberg Trials. Thirteen were found guilty and served short prison terms.

The DP camps in the US Zone, originally administered by the US military, were gradually being turned over to UNRRA personnel, who were specially trained and better equipped to run the camps, which the military management recognized. When I arrived at Camp Foehrenwald, the two organizations were working well together. The military director, a captain and combat man, was most cooperative in turning the camp over to UNRRA personnel.

The captain owned two Hungarian cavalry horses, the same breed of horses that I had ridden years before while visiting my cousins in Hungary. The captain invited me to ride with him, and many a time he and I galloped through the wide-open fields. The captain was quite a horseman and took excellent care of those magnificent specimens. Before returning to the United States, he bequeathed the horses to me. I continued to use the same stable and groom, who took good care of the horses, which I had named Jack and Jock. Later, when I was transferred to Camp Aschau, I had no way to take the horses with me. It took me quite some time to locate a vehicle to transport them to Camp Aschau. To my great surprise and regret, the animal transport arrived at Camp Aschau without the horses. There was only a note informing me that Jack and Jock had been exchanged for working horses for the camp. Unfortunately I did not possess any legal papers to prove my ownership.

The UNRRA staff at Camp Foehrenwald consisted of a Canadian Director, an American Deputy Director, a Czechoslovakian Principal Welfare Officer (the role assigned to me), a Dutch Assistant Welfare Officer, and an American Administrative Secretary. A doctor from New Zealand and a nurse from the US worked in the infirmary. Mrs. Henshaw, the Director, started to turn to me for advice on how to administer the camp, since she felt her assistant director was, in her words, "too weak." I enjoyed giving her my opinion on various matters, and the two of us formed an efficient working alliance. I was surprised at my administrative capabilities, which I did not know I possessed. It seemed to me that most of my advice was just good common sense.

My official assignment at the camp was to administer the program for the several hundred Jewish teenagers, most of whom were organized into kibbutz groups and hoped to emigrate to Israel, called Palestine at the time. These groups had remained together while traveling under precarious circumstances to the camp. They marched into Camp Foehrenwald three in a row, with the girls in the middle and the boys on both sides, protecting them. Many told gruesome stories of how they had been forced to beg on the streets or hide in woods and caves, leading a very deprived and disorganized life until they found each other and organized themselves, often with the help of adults who took them under their wing. Being part of a communal group gave the teenagers inner strength and helped them survive many obstacles, as did their idealism and strong desire to settle in Palestine against all odds.

Most of the young people were boys, I'm not sure why. Perhaps the living conditions had been too rigorous for some girls to manage.

There was a separate group of Orthodox Jewish teenagers called *yeshiva bochers*. *(Yeshiva* refers to the type of school they attended, and *bochers* means *boys*.) Their main interest was to attend an ultra-religious school and study the Torah. At the camp their studies were monitored by a famous Orthodox rabbi who was greatly revered by the ultra-Orthodox community. They too had a strong desire to settle in Palestine.

Some of the children at Camp Foehrenwald had unforgettable stories to tell. Lazy was a Polish teenager who had seen the Nazis shoot his parents simply because they were Jewish. He ran away in a panic and hid in the woods where he survived on berries. When it rained, he would sleep in the hayloft of a farm. The farmer found him and offered him a meal and a bed to stay the night. Lazy stayed on and had begun to recuperate when the farmer told him about a group of boys who were marching and singing along the highway. He asked the farmer to take him to the place where he had seen the boys. After observing them for a while from a distance, Lazy mustered enough courage to approach the group. The head of the group, careful not to let an impostor join their ranks, questioned him as to his identity as a Jew. Lazy passed the questioning with flying colors and after thanking the farmer for his help, joined the kibbutz group who were on their way to join a DP camp in Germany in order to emigrate to Palestine.

Then there was Ernest, a ten-year-old boy who saw his parents being carted off by the Nazis, never to be seen again. At that time he lived in Poland in a small town and had nowhere to turn, since the rest of his family lived in Warsaw. Ernest wandered around aimlessly until he came across a Catholic convent just outside town. He was exhausted and hungry. As he sat down to rest at the foot of the stairs at the entrance, the door opened and a nun beckoned him to enter. She gave him food and a bed to rest in and spoke to the Mother Superior, asking if he might stay. The nuns took in this sad and disheveled boy and hid him from the Nazis. He remained at the convent for several months, together with a few other Jewish children.

The I.G. Farben factory, located near the camp, was in the process of being dismantled of all the chemical substances they produced. The military government informed Mrs. Henshaw and me that some of the substances were highly sensitive to cold and should there be a frost, there might be an explosion. This was during the fall, so frost was a real possibility. To avoid anxious reactions, we did not share this knowledge with the rest of the staff. Instead we talked about how to proceed in case of an emergency evacuation. We asked each member of the team how they would go about accomplishing this rather frightening task. After some discussion, we agreed on a plan for handling a mass evacuation fast and efficiently. Fortunately all the chemical substances were removed before the first frost set in, and Mrs. Henshaw and

I breathed a huge sigh of relief. We were never told what sort of chemical substances were being removed.

After the captain left for the United States, a new group of officers, non-combat men, took over. It was Sukkot, the Jewish harvest festival, and the teenage population of the camp, my group, decided to thank the military government for liberating them. They marched the two miles to the local military headquarters, singing songs as they went. I marched with them. To our great dismay, the headquarters was surrounded by US soldiers pointing rifles and machine guns at us. I wound my way through the teenagers to the front of the line and asked what was going on. I was informed that the local Germans had warned the Americans that the DPs were coming to burn their houses down, along with the military headquarters. I was shocked and surprised, we all were, that the US government officials would listen to such a preposterous story, and I said as much to the officers in charge. Needless to say, the spirit of our group was crushed. They could hardly believe that the Germans could exercise such influence on the allied personnel. This hostile reception reactivated memories of the horrors most of them had so recently experienced. I was told that the DPs were not supposed to walk in groups outside the camp, a fact that was unknown to me. The event revealed the projections of the Germans. They themselves would have liked to burn down the buildings that housed the allied military.

The new head of the military government near Camp Foehrenwald, a major, came from a well-to-do family and was used to having his own way. He expected compliance from those around him, yet his administrative knowledge was sparse. When I dared to open my mouth and question his methodology in what I hoped was a benign and non-threatening manner, he became defensive. I also rejected his sexual advances and attempted to set some limits on his acting-out behavior. Without my knowledge, Major X decided to complain about me. He drove all the way to UNRRA headquarters in Frankfurt where he met with Gertrude Richmond and Connie Clark, the heads of the Child Welfare Department. Both thought his complaint to be questionable, so they called Mrs. Henshaw to ascertain my capabilities. Instead of a complaint, they received a glowing report of my administrative abilities, devotion, and integrity. And instead of the demotion that Major X probably had in mind, I was appointed Director of Camp Aschau by Mühldorf on the River Inn.

Pleased as I was with the promotion, I had a hard time leaving. I had formed good relationships with the staff, the madrichim (educators), and various camp leaders. Worst of all was leaving the children in the lurch, just when we were starting to build trust and develop some much-needed programs.

Mrs. Henshaw and most of her staff did not like to see me go, but there were two people who were glad—Major X and the Assistant Welfare Officer, whom I supervised. She was appointed Principal Welfare Officer by Major X, not for her administrative talents, which did not exist, but for the sexual favors she so generously bestowed upon him.

NOTE

1. *The Story of UNRRA*. Washington D.C.: Office of Public Information, 1948.

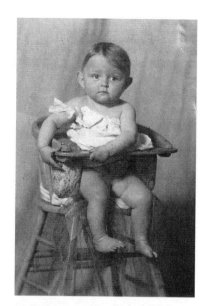

Myself as an infant.

My mother: Sidonie Brauch.

Mother, Father, myself, Martha.

Grandmother, Father, Aunt Paula, Uncle Filip.

General Eisenhower, Jean Henshaw, and Gertrude Steinova at Camp Foehrenwald.

UNRRA team for Camp Aschau.

Orthodox boys from the Mizrachi Kibbutz, Camp Aschau.

ORT garden project. Seeds brought from England.

ORT dressmaking class, Camp Aschau.

ORT metal shop, Camp Aschau.

Garden produce exhibition with head gardener on right, Camp Aschau.

Getting ready to dance the hora, Camp Aschau.

Aschau's sports team with trainer.

Eagle's Nest, Berchtesgarden.

Director of the Lambeth Children's Cottage and assistant.

The children of Lambeth Children's Cottage dressed up for acting out.

Erwin Pollitt.

Graduation at the University of Chicago.

Freud's couch and myself at the Center for Psychoanalytic Study.

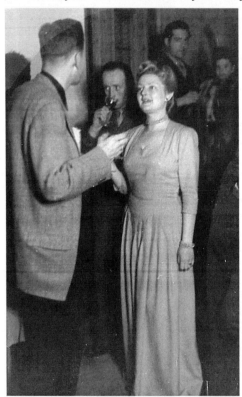

Me wearing ball gown made from a Nazi flag.

Chapter Seven

Camp Aschau

Camp Aschau by Mühldorf on the River Inn was a camp for displaced Jewish children, one of several camps administered by UNRRA Team 135. The area director was Colonel Wattleworth, who some months before had asked to have me on his team. Team 135 was sizable and multi-national. There were Lithuanian, Latvian, and Polish camps administered by an Australian Director, an American Deputy Director, a nurse from New Zealand, a doctor from Cuba, a Canadian Principle Welfare Officer, a Czech Welfare Officer, a Belgian Supply Officer, a French Messing Officer, and several more that I don't recall. Camp Aschau had, in addition to my position as Director, an American Administrative Secretary, a Dutch Supply Officer, a Norwegian Warehouse Officer, and, at my request, two Israeli workers, at that time called "Palestinian." We truly represented the United Nations with all these different nationalities speaking English and working for one cause—to help those destitute victims of war to help themselves.

Camp Aschau's Director, Barbara Donald, formerly an assistant to the journalist Walter Lippmann, was about to resign her post and return to the United States. There was to be an overlap of one month so that I could familiarize myself with the camp, its inhabitants, and Barbara Donald's administrative work.

SETTLING IN

Barbara Donald and I quickly developed a close friendship. We were up late every night discussing all sorts of subjects. On her way back to the United States, she stopped at the US Embassy in London in an attempt to sort out the mix-up regarding my visa for emigration to the United States. She discovered that the embassy was holding two files on me, one under "Gertrude Stein" and another under "Gertrude Steinova." The latter name had been given to me by the Czech Government when they signed me up to work with the United Nations. More of this later.

Ordinarily UNRRA teams did not live at the camps they supervised but traveled to each camp daily. My suggestion to my staff was that we move into Camp Aschau as soon as possible because the children and adults would feel much safer with us there both day and night. This decision became more urgent because the German population was quite hostile to the Jews who populated the camp. They had destroyed the little chapel outside the camp, blaming the Jews for this vandalism. The US Central Intelligence Corps started to investigate the inhabitants of the camp but soon determined that the Germans were responsible.

We could not move in without furniture, which we did not possess. Any military person was given the authority to requisition necessary objects from the German economy, provided they had been owned by someone in the Nazi regime. I therefore got in touch with the German mayor of Aschau by Mühldorf, and he led me to houses of well-known Nazi party officials for me to pick furniture for our billet. This was a task I did not enjoy. To enter someone's home and pick a piece of furniture from the living room was a deed I found disturbing. Picking a couch in one home, an easy chair in another, and a bed in still another was what I attempted to do. The idea was to spread the furniture hunt around in order to limit the pain of dispossession. Needless to say, I was treated with contempt and not-so-hidden hostility by those families and by the mayor who, though superficially polite, was a Nazi himself. Nevertheless, I did collect a nice lot of sturdy and well designed furniture for our billet, and we moved in.

The billet that housed the staff consisted of a living room, a dining room, two bedrooms, a well-equipped kitchen, a bathroom, and a toilet by the main entrance, all connected by a long, large hall. On the other side of the house, with a separate entrance, there were several bedrooms, a living room, and a bathroom. Barbara Donald and I lived in the half of the building containing the kitchen, while the rest of the staff lived in the other half. When Barbara Donald left, I occupied our part of the house by myself.

One cold winter's night well after midnight I heard someone in the tiled hall of the building walking slowly and deliberately towards my room. I was terrified. Since we were a civilian agency, we were not allowed to possess guns. A dress sword I had purchased hung over my bed, but it was useless as a weapon. While the steps were coming slowly closer and closer down the long hall, I jumped out of the window in my nightgown and ran to the other front door. I rang the bell, but there was no reply. Apparently everyone was fast asleep. In my anxiety I banged with my fist against the small glass window of the door, which I managed to break, causing blood to run down my arms from the deep cuts I had incurred. The Dutch Supply Officer awoke and let me in and from that night on I slept in the room next door to his. The next day we found footprints from what looked like a man's shoes on the outside wall of the house. Evidently he had pulled himself up by the ledge and entered through the small open window of the toilet. We all agreed that this incident was an attempt to frighten me. I often wondered whether my requisitioning Nazi furniture had something to do with it.

For our protection I purchased a trained bloodhound from one of the farmers. This dog had drooping ears, sad eyes, and a terrible bark. I named him Flip and became quite attached to him. He lived outdoors in a wooden hut, was all skin and bones, and consumed a tremendous amount of food until he looked less emaciated. Flip could be fierce. While under our care, he attacked a deer and left it in such a bad state that it had to be euthanized. When I returned from a leave in London, Flip had disappeared. I discovered that he now belonged to an officer in the US Army. While I was in London, his original owner had called Flip back with a whistle, starved him once again, and then resold him, this time to the military man. This was another of my early impressions of the local German population.

Ora Markstein, a sculptor currently living in Hamilton, Canada, spent a year in Camp Aschau and had her baby there. She vividly remembers the hostility of one particular German farmer. Desperate for some fresh vegetables to feed to her infant son, she and her mother approached a farmer who had two fierce-looking German shepherds on leashes. Over the dogs' frantic barking, she asked if he would sell her some fresh spinach. He refused and shouted at the dogs, "Go! Kill them!" To Ora's surprise, the farmer did not let the dogs off their leashes. Fortunately this was an empty threat. "That night after dark," Ora added, "my husband and I left camp and stole some carrots and a few handfuls of spinach from the farmer's field."[1]

Aschau by Muehldorf on the River Inn was a small sleepy village in Bavaria, about an hour's drive by the autobahn from Munich. The River Inn, which originates in Switzerland, enters Austria, crosses the border into Bavaria, ambles along the border between Germany and Austria, and flows into the Danube at Passau. The camp, like Camp Foehrenwald, was once a workers' camp for the I.G. Farben company. Before we arrived, it was inhabited by US Army personnel who painted all the buildings a drab khaki color. The physical plant was well planned and served the displaced and orphaned children very well, with its central heating system, well equipped kitchen, central bath house, community hall, and many barracks. Each of these had a living room, a bedroom which housed six to eight children, a bathroom with several wash basins, and a room for the madrich (educator). One of the buildings served as an infirmary staffed by a Polish doctor and a Lithuanian nurse who attended to minor physical problems. The administrative buildings were converted into schools, workshops, UNRRA offices, and recreation halls. Camp

Aschau was not as large as the other children's centers, thus enabling the staff to have a more personal relationship with the children.

Although the camp had supposedly been cleared of all the ammunition that was haphazardly lying around, there was one shell that had been overlooked. Unfortunately one of the boys played with it and it blew up in his face, causing him the loss of one eye. There were many muddy spaces sprawled around the camp, and the khaki colored buildings were quite depressing. I had the entire camp repainted in light cheerful colors, which helped to lift everyone's spirits. I was nearly court-martialed for spending too much money but managed to talk my way out of it at a hearing by emphasizing the psychological and emotional needs of the children.

THE CHILDREN

While Barbara Donald was Director, the camp was half empty, but more and more people arrived and soon the camp was filled to capacity not with laughter but with the great needs of a group of about four hundred severely deprived children. Along with the children were two hundred adults, most of whom were madrichim, who comprised some of the workforce of the camp.

When we met the children's transports at the train station, we brought food with us. Hungry, disheveled, neglected, and severely depressed groups of children awaited our welcome. There was a group of eleven children who came from Poland with two adults, former high school teachers who were also fleeing from the Nazis. The adults had taken the children under their wing and supervised them on their way to Germany. Amongst them was a family of four, a brother and three sisters whose parents had been carted off by the Nazis to a concentration camp. If it were not for the brother, the oldest family member, the girls would not have survived. The brother had helped to hide the girls in the woods and in caves and had provided them with food until the two teachers met them by chance and took over, much to the children's relief.

This group of children came from a well-to-do, well-educated family. While staying at Camp Aschau, Edith, the oldest sister, became very ill and had to be hospitalized in Munich. The diagnosis was a brain tumor and the doctors recommended a brain specialist in Bochum, a town in the British Zone. I had the authority in an emergency to order a plane through the local military government and did so. The camp doctor, one of the high school teachers, the camp nurse, Edith, and I boarded the small plane and flew to Bochum in the British Zone of Germany. We were housed in the hospital and told to keep our doors locked to avoid having a nurse enter our room and shave off the hair from our heads. We were fed a steady diet of cabbage and potato soup, which was all they had, even for the patients and the staff. It was very sad to hear Edith's final diagnosis—sarcoma on the brain. It had metastasized, much to everyone's dismay. The doctor, the nurse, and I flew back to Aschau, leaving the high school teacher with Edith to comfort her during the few days she had left of her short life. Edith was thirteen years old.

One of the last transports to arrive at Aschau was a group of young children from Hungary. They suffered from malnutrition and were dressed in rags—a very deprived and despondent group. Most of them were religious kids belonging to the Mizrachi movement. These children came from small towns and villages which had a large proportion of Orthodox Jews. One of the madrichim showed me his overcoat. He had sewn all his paper money in between the cloth and the lining. I had no idea of the worth of the pengö, the Hungarian currency, but assumed that his money was as worthless as the German mark.

Another group of children arrived who had been forced to leave two other camps because of their unruly behavior. These children, together with their parents, had fled from Poland to Russia, where anti-Semitic Soviet authorities sent them to Siberia. Most of the parents died, partly because of the severe weather and partly because of the lack of aid the USSR extended to them. The children formed a gang and survived by stealing, conniving, and living in caves or in the woods and off the land. These children did not know what a toilet was. On their first day at Camp Aschau they stole the camp's entire coal supply and hoarded it behind their barracks. They also stole other children's toys. Their life experience had taught them to trust no one lest they be annihilated. They did not have an adult with them, and we had to find madrichim to help them settle down to the everyday living conditions and standards of the camp.

There were very few children under eight years of age at the camp because many younger children had not survived the rigorous living conditions. Many of those who did survive had been in concentration camps, had seen their parents shoved into gas chambers, and themselves had undergone severe deprivation and mistreatment. Needing so much for so long, they developed a number of defense mechanisms. They were independent and adult-like in a pathetic sort of way because they had been forced to age prematurely. When they first arrived, if you tried to give them something, they would refuse, considering it shameful to accept any favor, gift, or even necessity. Their dependency longings had been walled off, suppressed, repressed, and displaced since their living conditions demanded the bare struggle for survival. When finally faced with some protected care at the camp, their needs became overwhelming to them and they became very demanding of what they thought were their rights. This aggressiveness represented a healthy defense that had kept them going through adversity. Simultaneously, they revealed a paranoid quality. They were quick to sense danger and act on it, and it was this very paranoia that often had made the difference between life and death. The extremely traumatizing experiences they had undergone had shattered their basic trust.

This demanding and aggressive attitude was also prevalent in most of the adults. The madrichim of some of the self-appointed kibbutz group leaders would come to my office and pound their fists on my desk demanding better quality food and basic necessities. At first we were unable to fulfill their demands for such things as fresh foods, especially fruits and vegetables, nor did we have some of the bare necessities such as toothbrushes, toothpaste, and combs. Nor did the clothes, mostly army uniforms, meet everyone's needs. We received one Red Cross package per person through UNRRA, which mainly contained dehydrated food. Unable to tolerate this food, a delegation arrived at our mess hall, placed a tray of food before us, and said, "Eat that slop yourselves." They did not realize that we had to eat the same food ourselves and agreed that it was inadequate, so inadequate that I ended up at an army hospital for a short time with a vitamin deficiency. Subsequently we employed a nutritionist who helped the cooks prepare the dehydrated food in a more appetizing way.

The only currency on the German market was cigarettes. The German mark was practically worthless, as were the USA printed occupation dollars. These had purchasing power only at the local PX, the military supply store for US forces, which we had the privilege to use. Officially we were not allowed to purchase any kind of food from the German economy, but in order to obtain fresh meat, we purchased a cow every week by paying with cigarettes. The cows were slaughtered by a religious butcher called a "shechet." During an inspection by one of the UNRRA officers, we explained our need for a milk cow, based on the infants and small children in the camp who had to have milk in order to survive. We hoped that the UNRRA officers would not notice that our cow kept changing colors.

Since nearly everyone in the camp had been deprived of adequate food, the need for good meals was paramount. Everyone wanted to work in the kitchen, hoping to get some extra food, and bloody battles ensued over the recruitment of the kitchen staff regarding who could cook, serve food, and wash dishes. In the end the kitchen was staffed by the Mizrachi group and as a result the whole camp population enjoyed kosher food.

BRINGING IN SUPPLIES

Using cigarettes as bartering tender, I purchased cattle manure which was spread all along the inside of the air raid shelter that ran along one side of the camp, and we grew mushrooms. While on leave in England, I purchased seeds, and we planted lettuce, tomatoes, carrots, and other vegetables. Every bare spot in the camp was used for this project and soon the camp looked like a big garden. A number of Hungarian children and adolescents who had grown up on farms became the camp gardeners and did an excellent job.

On my weekly visits to Munich, I contacted the American Jewish Joint Distribution Committee (AJDC) who helped a great deal in providing various food products to supplement our diet. This was a creative undertaking, since I knew of no other camp that made use of this resource. It was left up to the adult displaced persons population to barter on the black market in order to supplement their diet.

My ability to travel to Munich every week was facilitated by the assignment of several vehicles to our camp from UNRRA Team 135. We received three weapons carriers, three jeeps, and one car. A Hungarian auto mechanic taught me to drive on one of the weapons carriers, with its energy-absorbing necessity to double clutch. This was the vehicle I used most often to travel to Munich because it was large enough to carry a week's supplies. For other trips I sometimes drove a jeep but much preferred driving the car, a large bright red Mercedes Benz, well equipped for those days and upholstered with black patent leather. It was stunning! It was my guess that this car had belonged to one of the top echelon Nazi officials. Unfortunately the car was not to be mine for long. During an inspection from headquarters, one of the UNRRA bigwigs spotted the car and requisitioned it for himself.

MARCHING

Many of the groups, having lived under military conditions and severe regimentation, started to march around the camp. It was this marching that had kept the groups together while wandering all over Europe in order to come to the camp. The marching represented in part an identification with the aggressor, since the SS and other Nazi groups did this very marching in every town and village, to show off their discipline and intimidate the bystanders. Marching also gave the children a feeling of power, security, and unity with their group. Every morning at six o'clock marches were conducted around the camp. There were three rows, with the girls in the middle and everyone dressed in dark trousers or skirts with white shirts and blouses. As they marched, the children sang concentration camp songs. The singing and marching provided great relief from all their suffering and kept up the spirit of the group.

Each group had a sign displaying its name for all to see. There was the Mizrachi group which was Orthodox, the Agudah group which was ultra Orthodox, the Hashomer Hatzair group which represented a more socialistic philosophy, and a fourth group, called Kadima, which was somewhere in between. During the first three months as they settled into camp, these groups maintained their own separate identity and did not mix in with the others.

PROGRAMS

We started an educational program whereby each child attended school for half a day and undertook a work program for the rest of the day. The school program was designed to teach basic subjects such as English, Hebrew, mathematics, and geography. I designed a certificate, which we issued at the end of each semester. It was difficult to find qualified teachers, but there were a few. Since most of the children were preparing for emigration to Palestine, we focused our program on meeting their aims. We even had a yeshiva for the Orthodox boys and a library with about 750 books.

We had asked to have two officers from the Palestinian government assigned to Camp Aschau. We received one who represented views and beliefs close to those of the Hashomer Hatzair kibbutz while the other came from the Mizrachi movement. Both Palestinians worked closely with the children and madrichim, educating them on the customs and mores of their chosen land, Palestine. They taught them Hebrew and in general provided them with an excellent educational background.

Most of the workshops were organized by ORT (Organization for Training and Rehabilitation), a worldwide Jewish organization that had a branch in Munich which sent us two instructors, upon my request. One workshop prepared the youngsters to become tailors or dressmakers, trades that were useful in most countries. Another workshop was conducted by our chief mechanic and driver, the Hungarian displaced person who had taught me to drive. With the help of his students, he disassembled a jeep only to reassemble it again. This was a popular course, and he was an excellent teacher. There was an American soldier stationed nearby who also disassembled a jeep—for the purpose of shipping it home to the US, piece by piece. He was caught at his last shipment through the APO (Army Post Office) and was punished.

Another workshop was made up of the Hungarian gardeners who grew and harvested vegetables for the inhabitants of the camp. A fourth workshop taught tool making. On my travels I discovered a factory with excellent machinery and equipment for the production of metal tools. I requisitioned the equipment, and we hired a toolmaker from ORT who taught the youngsters how to produce tools from steel and brass. This was a highly specialized undertaking and served us very well. In addition to tools, the children produced menorahs which one can purchase in Israel to this day. The special design of these menorahs indicates that they originally came from Camp Aschau.

We decided to open the camp for an exhibition of the products of the workshops. Many UNRRA officers and dignitaries from other organizations attended this event. We showed off our metal products and our garden produce, some of which was grown inside bottles. We designated a hall for the exhibition and decorated it with white and blue blankets from a shipment we had received from the AJDC. The exhibit proved to be a great success and a good time was had by all.

GOVERNING

All major decisions at the camp were discussed with the camp committee. This group, at first appointed and later elected, was made up primarily of madrichim. The same pattern was followed by my staff, with all administrative decisions being discussed, evaluated, and voted upon. We put in long hours and cooperated well with each other for the welfare of our displaced persons. There were many cultural differences among us, but these did not interfere with our accomplishing the tasks at hand. UNRRA Team 135, with its nationally diverse personnel, also worked well together, but there was one major difference of opinion. The British nationals, going along with the official policy of their government, unanimously agreed that the Jewish displaced persons should not be allowed to emigrate to Palestine. The area director, Colonel Wattleworth, felt especially strongly in this regard. I kept my opinion to myself and waited not too patiently for a chance to act upon it.

One of my more bothersome duties involved reassuring the "police," teenagers who were expected to act as night watchmen. The camp was surrounded by a high wire fence which local farmers tried to dismantle and steal on several occasions. Often while on patrol, our young policemen would be frightened by shadows and noises at the edge of camp and would wake me up in the middle of the night. Sometimes my words would be enough to reassure them, but frequently I had to get up and see for myself what was going on.

In order to arrange some sort of reward for the workers at the camp, we designed a point system, patterned on the rationing of food in England, enabling them to purchase necessities such as toilet articles and cigarettes at the local canteen. This represented their salaries, much to their satisfaction.

We also appointed ministers of food, culture, employment, and education, to name a few, patterned after the British parliamentary system, to help run the camp by the people and for the people, all of which worked very well. The population of the camp acknowledged that they could govern themselves with some help from UNRRA. Doing so gave them a sense of responsibility and feelings of self-worth.

END OF MARCHING

The various kibbutz groups at Camp Aschau finally stopped marching. Instead, every afternoon after dinner, everyone formed two large circles, one inside the other, and danced the hora while singing various Hebrew and Israeli songs. From time to time they leapt into the air as if they were one body. Their basic needs were being met, they participated in a predictable program of work, study, and recreation, they were treated with dignity and respect, and they were included in the decision-making process. Feeling secure, they began to trust people again. They had come to realize that this was their camp. They experienced unity of purpose, since they were convinced that migrating to Palestine was their ultimate goal, a goal they could actually achieve.

As their emotional wounds started to heal and they began to develop feelings of security, their spirits soared. They regarded the camp as theirs to be managed and participated in, and individual members began to invest themselves in the community. A boot repair shop cropped up, manned by a few children and adolescents who wanted to give of themselves and who knew the trade, having been apprenticed in Poland. For the first time shoes were repaired and preserved. A sports team was formed and Camp Aschau won first prize in a zone-wide competition in soccer and light athletics.

Puppet shows sprang up as if from nowhere, to the delight of the children of all ages. The first, called "Peter and the Snowman," involved a great deal of audience participation and had Peter and his friend the Snowman chasing the Wicked Witch all over the globe. The person who wrote, produced, and directed the puppet shows was Jancsi Hirsch, a Hungarian teenager who knew at the age of five that he wanted to be a theater director when he grew up. Jancsi had lost his brother and both parents in Auschwitz and had lived through the horrors of the Budapest ghetto, but he never lost sight of his dream. In 1947 he emigrated to Canada, changed his name to John Hirsch, completed his education, and became one of Canada's most distinguished theater directors. To name a few highlights of his career, he was co-founder and artistic director of the Manitoba Theatre Centre, drama director for the Canadian Broadcasting Company, and artistic director of the Stratford Festival.

Camp Aschau was a pleasant place to be. Marianne Guttmann, a close friend of John Hirsch and the set designer for the puppet shows, described it like this:

> I often thought what a beautiful place Camp Aschau was. Its pastel colored buildings were situated on the rolling hillocks of the camp and from these grassy hillocks rose on three sides the forested mountains that we climbed in summer and in winter. ...The various groups got along very well and I remem-

ber my stay in UNRRA Children's Centre Aschau as rich in work and fun, in camaraderie and in opportunities to mature. Life in Aschau was a unique experience, one that ordinary adolescent life would not have given me.[2]

To do some bragging, under my supervision and administration, Camp Aschau was regarded as the best organized and most successful children's camp in the US Zone.

SUPERVISION

While I was Director of Camp Aschau, I was appointed supervisor of five other DP camps as well. The first was a farm manned by White Russians. The farm was run democratically by an elected council whose members worked very well with each other and with the administration. Visiting this camp was a pleasure. There were crops growing in the fields and cows grazing in the meadows. The men greeted us warmly and fed us well with dairy products and fresh produce from the farm. They often invited us to take part in their festivities where they sang Russian folk songs and taught us Russian dances. I remember one Russian Christmas celebration where I ate so much I wasn't hungry for the next three days. We found out later that these hospitable men were not displaced persons in the usual sense but deserters from the Russian Army.

The second camp assigned to me was Camp Traunstein, a beautifully situated Jewish children's camp in close proximity to the Austrian border. Two other children's camps I supervised were Camp Rosenheim near Prien am Chiemsee, well run by Greta Fischer, an experienced welfare officer who happened to be the sister of a good friend of mine. Like me, Greta Fischer was a Czech citizen representing the Czech Government in Exile. The fourth children's center under my supervision was called Kloster Indersdorf. This was a monastery which housed infants and children looked after primarily by nuns, who took good care of them.

Camp Rosenheim provided the background in the film *The Search*, featuring Jarmila Novotná, Ivan Jandl, Montgomery Clift, and children from nearby DP camps, including Camp Aschau. Winner of Academy Awards for Best Story and a special award for "the outstanding juvenile performance of 1948," *The Search* tells the true story of a mother who searched for her son in various DP camps and eventually found him.

RESETTLEMENT PROGRAM

One of the first countries to open its doors to displaced persons was Canada. They took in a great many adults of Baltic and Polish nationalities who were willing to work in the coal mines. And Great Britain accepted 150 Jewish Orthodox children to live in foster homes with Jewish Orthodox families. In Camp Aschau we started the process of registering the children who were interested in joining this migration, but a group of adults broke into our offices and destroyed the original registration forms. This vandalism was initiated by a Munich-based "Miracle Rabbi" who ruled that these children should go to Palestine instead. His followers, a very conservative Orthodox group, acted upon his command. I had to smuggle these children out of Camp Aschau during the night and move them to another children's center where we reprocessed their applications. Interesting to note, this very Miracle Rabbi himself emigrated not to Palestine but to the USA.

One possibility for migrating to Palestine was through Aliyah Bet, an underground movement organized by Haganah, the Palestinian secret service, with the cooperation of the Palestinian Agency, an organization representing the Jews in Palestine. I was recruited by Haganah to aid the Aliyah Bet, specifically to help Jewish children emigrate to Palestine. This was a hush-hush illegal operation unbeknownst to the regular UNRRA staff. Since I worked well with the Palestinian representatives at Camp Aschau and was able to preserve confidentiality, Haganah trusted me in a role which I was honored to fulfill.

Haganah, with my approval, decided to turn the Traunstein camp into an assembly center from which children were escorted over the Austrian border. From there they had to travel through rough and mountainous territory to Marseille, France, where a boat was waiting to transport them to Palestine. The children, accompanied by their madrichim, came from DP camps all over the US Zone, including Camp Aschau. They had been somewhat prepared before leaving their original camp but underwent further training at Traunstein by Palestinian representatives who thoroughly briefed them on the dangers and obstacles they would encounter. The children, loaded down with food and warm clothing, left quietly with our blessing, and another group of children took their place. It was a smooth, efficiently run operation. The official reports we presented from the camp were like those from the other children's camps, and with closed lips we reported the number of inhabitants that would enable us to receive the right amount of food and medical supplies.

One day I received notice that a group of US congressmen sent by President Truman would arrive at Camp Traunstein, one of the camps I supervised. The purpose of their visit was to ascertain why so many displaced children had failed to emigrate. The impending visit was anxiety provoking for me, but at least I had some time to prepare the camp and its inhabitants for the visit. I asked the military rabbi, who knew what the purpose of the camp was, to come to my aid should I make a slip and jeopardize the whole operation. Officially the military government in the American Zone took the same view as the British. Unofficially they shut their eyes and did not interfere, since fewer displaced persons meant fewer mouths to feed.

The meeting started and ended without any flip-flops or *faux pas*. The congressmen asked many pertinent questions which I was able to answer to their satisfaction. I emphasized the need for countries to open their doors to those deprived Jewish children who so far had not managed to find a permanent home. Not long after the delegation's visit, the United States allowed 450 children, Jewish and non-Jewish, to emigrate to the United States on a non-quota basis. Among them were a handful of children from Camp Aschau. I hope the meeting I held with the congressmen contributed to the decision.

As time went by and most of the inhabitants of Camp Aschau had failed to emigrate, their spirit took a nosedive. Countries that opened their door to DPs always specified what kind of DPs they wanted and perhaps in part because of lingering anti-Semitism, the countries almost never wanted Jews. The children and adults at Camp Aschau felt that they were the forgotten people, forgotten by the very ones who had liberated them from oppression. Many of the non-Jewish displaced persons had not suffered as much and consequently were far less demanding of what they considered to be their needs and rights. This does not deny the fact that other nationalities had to undergo great hardships in labor camps or concentration camps. Nevertheless, the Jewish groups presented more of a problem to the US authorities because relatively more Jews had undergone the extreme concentration camp experiences.

Perhaps because of the success in moving small groups of children to Palestine, Haganah and the Palestinian Agency decided to rent a large boat and send a large group to Palestine, thus defying British rule. The children from Camp Aschau were prepared, to the best of our abilities, psychologically, emotionally, and economically to migrate to Palestine. We gave them warm clothing, packaged food, and medical supplies. In the middle of the night most of the camp became empty while the children and their madrichim left for the *Exodus*, the famous ship that everyone has heard about from the book by Leon Uris and the movie by the same name. In spite of the trying and exhausting experiences these youngsters faced on the *Exodus*, they did not break down as the British authorities had expected, and, with the aid and encouragement of the Palestinian Agency and Haganah, did ultimately arrive at their destination. It is my contention that their strong ego, healthy aggression, persistence, and general personality make-up helped this bold plan to succeed.

In spite of my need to fudge facts and resort to some white lies and fancy juggling acts, aiding and helping these children was a most gratifying and rewarding experience. I feel I have lived the history of Palestine, or rather

Israel, and have contributed in a small way to the development and acceptance of Israel. I feel privileged and proud to have had this opportunity.

TIME OUT

The UNRRA staff worked hard and also played hard. We had a number of parties which we all thoroughly enjoyed. These parties were held not only for the entire UNRRA team but also for military personnel. Wearing a uniform all the time became tedious. Consequently, for one of these events I decided to appear in an evening gown. I found a German dressmaker willing to sew for me in exchange for cigarettes. It was not easy to obtain fabric right after the war, but my dressmaker found a Nazi flag and made me quite an impressive gown, which I wore to the delight of many.

SURVIVORS

It is interesting to note that most of the people interviewed by Steven Spielberg in 1996 in Chicago presented some pathology related to their traumatic experiences due to the Nazi atrocities. I myself was interviewed by the Steven Spielberg group. My interview, in abbreviated form, landed in the *Chicago Tribune.* From that day on I became a telephone therapist. Many people who had been traumatized by the Nazis called me and talked at length about their experiences, only to hang up at the conclusion of our talk never to be heard from again. They did not want anyone else to know about their experiences and had not even shared them with their own children.

One of the interviewers presented a paper on the perceptions of the Holocaust victims and said that many of them were fearful of allowing their offspring to stay away from home for any length of time without checking back with them. They became overprotective parents with some paranoid tendencies. Another study I am familiar with was made in Great Britain showing that the children who were evacuated to the countryside or to Canada when the bombing of London began were much worse off emotionally than those who remained at home in London with their parents. Family ties enabled those children to endure the hardships of the London Blitz.

All the children who survived the Holocaust experience had strong egos. In my opinion, they had a secure early childhood with consistent good care by the primary caretaker. Because they had a secure, nurturing early childhood, the basic ability to survive was built into their personality development.

One interesting aspect of the conscious and preconscious development that preceded their Holocaust experiences was that most of the children had a strong superego. Many of the children who were in concentration camps became very religious. Some even became religious fanatics. Their religious beliefs enabled them to transcend their severe depression and deprivation and kept them alive.

Moshe, a madrich and member of the governing board at Camp Aschau, told me about his imprisonment in a concentration camp. He had been forced to watch his mother being pushed into a gas chamber and saw his father shot without provocation by one of the guards. Moshe survived, and, together with a number of his inmates, became very religious. By praying to God, he found some relief and the ability to endure. He, together with his soul mates, presented a tough front. Something else that kept him alive was taking food from the mouths of dead people.

In my opinion, most concentration camp survivors have to deal with an emotional scar, which today we would call post-traumatic stress disorder, for the duration of their lives. This also holds true for the children who had to undergo separation from their families, loss of their families, and the consequent traumatic experiences. They too were dealt a blow, which by its very nature leaves a permanent emotional scar. In spite of the severe traumas they were exposed to, the great majority of them managed to lead productive lives.[3]

TRAVEL

As I traveled from one camp to the next, I drove along roads in close proximity to the Alps. The mountains are awe-inspiring. Since the main rock of the Alps consists of calcium, they are basically white, but change color as they reflect different rays from the sun. From yellow to orange to red and pink, from pink to mauve to violet and blue—this is the range of colors reflected from the sunlight on the Alps, depending on the time of day. After living amidst rubble both during and after the war, I found it soothing to be among these mountains, in a part of the world that bombs had not destroyed.

In the summertime the cattle grazed in the lush meadows near the top of the mountains, but in the fall they were herded down to the valleys in order to avoid the harsh winters at the higher altitudes. For this special occasion the herd master dressed the best-looking cows in paper crowns of yellow, pink, and orange and put colorful paper chains around their bodies. With the crowned cows in front, the herd marched in a dignified manner—a sight to behold. The clanging of the cow bells echoed through the mountain range. It took little effort for the master and dogs to keep the herd together, and it looked to me as if the cows themselves were aware of the importance of the occasion.

During my sojourn in the US Zone of Germany, I was able to visit some interesting vacation and sightseeing spots. My close friend Vera, who was an

UNRRA officer from Canada, and I ventured to stay at Garmisch-Partenkir-
chen, one of Germany's most picturesque Alpine resorts, where the CIC
(Counter Intelligence Corps, later to become the CIA) had their headquarters.
To stay there over the weekend in an elegant hotel cost us only three cartons
of cigarettes. Vera and I also traveled to Oberammergau, another interesting
town, famous for performing Passion Plays. The theater, which is very old
and very large, has great acoustics. From the back row, one can hear a pin
drop on the stage. There was no performance when we were there. The actor
who was to play Jesus Christ—a known Nazi—had to go through a de-
Nazification process by the military government before the play could go on.

One of my traveling companions was Lily Lipman, a teacher and AJDC
member from Johannesburg, South Africa. Lily's parents had left Russia for
Johannesburg because of the pogroms of the Jews. Lily, who had been born
in South Africa, wanted me to emigrate there, an invitation which I declined
primarily because I did not want to live in a country which practiced apart-
heid. When Lily visited me in Chicago in the seventies, she had earned a
Ph.D. in education and had become the principal of a high school.

Our first trip together was to the Eagle's Nest in Berchtesgarden. This
was where Hitler received all the foreign dignitaries. The Eagle's Nest was
located high on a mountain at the end of a road full of hairpin turns. The
inclines were so steep that ordinary cars couldn't make it, only jeeps. By the
time we arrived, all the furniture had been removed and we faced bare walls
in this somewhat creepy place. Below the elevator there was a space which
enabled one of Hitler's henchmen to listen in on what the visitors were
saying on their way up to and down from their meeting.

Lily and I also visited Vienna, much to my distress. All the old memories
came flooding back when I visited my home. I rang the bell to our former
flat, but no one answered. I rang the bell to the ground floor apartment of the
concierge, who had been so kind to me when I was a child. He opened his
door and rather than inviting us in, stepped out. He looked older and was no
longer wearing his swastika armband. I was wearing my UNRRA uniform
which identified me as a captain in the American army and it occurred to me
that he might not recognize me.

"Remember me?" I asked. "I'm Gertrude Stein."

The concierge looked panic-stricken. He said nothing and fixed his eyes
firmly on the ground.

I asked him what had happened to my family. He said nothing but
squirmed uncomfortably, like a little child who has done a bad deed. I asked
if he would let me into our former flat. Again he did not reply.

It was obvious to me what had happened. It was he who had betrayed my
family, identifying them as Jews and turning them over to the Nazi authorities.

At the time of this visit, Vienna was divided into Russian, British, French, and American Zones. Since there was a large international military conference being held there, Lily and I were unable to find a room and had to leave after being there for only a day, which was fine with me. I vowed never to return.

I frequently traveled to Prague, since most of my Czech embassy friends had returned to Czechoslovakia, taking up their former positions. I met and visited with various ministers, including Dr. Eric Seiler, the Minister of Health and Social Welfare who had so generously sponsored my training in London. A good friend of mine from back in London who was now the secretary to the Secretary of State showed me the office of the President in the Hradschin Castle with its magnificent view over Prague, a beautiful medieval city that had not been bombed in the war. My friend arranged for me to have a limousine and a driver who showed me most of the historical places in Prague and the surrounding areas. This grand reception made me feel like a VIP and I was most grateful for my friend's generosity. Whenever I was in Prague, I stayed at the Alcron Hotel, the oldest and most elegant hotel in town, on Wenceslas Square. When tourists lined up at the reception desk to be assigned a room, I was called aside and assigned the elegant bridal suite—another luxury arranged for me by my friend.

On one of these visits I decided to visit my father's hometown in Bohemia. My driver and I drove south for many miles before arriving at our destination. Nestled among rolling hills and well maintained fields, Novy Oetting was a small, sleepy little village with charming painted window shutters and differently colored houses. It looked like a stage set for a performance of Smetana's *The Bartered Bride* except that in this village the flowers in the windows, blooming profusely, were real. Much to my delight, the Buergermeister, a dignified old gentleman, remembered my paternal family and expressed fond feelings for them. He told me that my family was highly regarded in the community. This visit had a great deal of meaning for me. I was amazed to find someone still alive who had known my family.

I undertook my last visit to Prague in order to revalidate my passport. This time I traveled by train. When I arrived at the border, a Czech liaison officer looked at my passport and suggested that I stay the night in Germany. It was evening, and I decided to take his advice. When I woke up the next morning, I found out, much to my horror, that the Communists had taken over Czechoslovakia. The liaison officer knew what he was doing when he advised me to stay in Germany. If I had gone into Czechoslovakia, I would not have been allowed to leave and might even have been imprisoned. From the border town I made arrangements to fly to London and had my passport revalidated there. When I returned to Germany, rumor had it amongst the displaced persons camps that I must be a Communist because I traveled to Czechoslovakia. It took some time to dispel this myth.

After the Communists took over the Czechoslovakian government, I received a letter from Dr. Eric Seiler informing me that he and his wife needed to leave the country and asking if I would be willing to help them. I felt bad for them that their lives were at risk and glad that I was given an opportunity to help. The plan was that he and his wife would leave all their belongings behind and walk through the woods where there were no Russian guards, across to the German border where I would have a car waiting to bring them to my billet. We carefully planned this move, taking some risks, which one always has to do under such circumstances. The meeting point was free of guards, and I breathed a happy sigh of relief when I spotted Dr. Seiler and his wife walking towards me through the woods with their suitcases. I put them into our housing unit, explaining little to the staff other than that they had come to visit me. I arranged for them to have papers proving them to be displaced persons, which in fact they were. This made it easier for them to travel to Canada where they planned to make their new home.

Dr. Seiler and his wife arrived safely in Montreal and I continued to be in touch with them by mail for many years until his death. Dr. Seiler was a lawyer by profession but could not practice Roman law in Canada and instead went into business, at which he was quite successful. His wife did not work but gave him a great deal of emotional support. We had an amicable relationship all along, based on mutual concern and respect. He died of a heart attack most unexpectedly, which came as a shock to all of us.

Another memorable trip I undertook was to Amsterdam. Although I was wearing my UNRRA uniform, the Dutch border authorities once again suspected me of being a spy. Not satisfied with dumping everything out of my expensive new leather and metal suitcase, they took a razor blade to it and cut it into pieces to see if anything was hidden in the lining.

IRO TAKES OVER

By 1947 the political atmosphere had changed considerably. Nations in the Soviet bloc had dropped out of UNRRA, and UNRRA came to an end. The IRO (International Refugee Organization) took over with a reduced budget and staff. Only about seventeen countries remained involved, considerably reducing the scope of the programs. Half of the UNRRA staff members were dismissed. I was promoted to Major and given a different assignment. All of the healthy children from Camp Aschau had emigrated. For a while the camp was empty but later became an ORT training center for emotionally and physically disabled adolescents from all over the US Zone.

My job was now almost exclusively administrative. No longer working with the children in the camps, I was dealing mainly with the elected camp directors and the administrative staffs and was responsible for about 45,000 displaced persons in all. On one occasion I led a staff meeting in Traunstein for all the IRO personnel in the American Zone, outlining the rules and regulations and all possible chances for displaced persons to emigrate to the USA, Canada, and South America as well as to various countries in Europe.

At the Yalta Conference American, British, and Russian leaders agreed that UNRRA and later IRO personnel had to arrange for the respective liaison officers to visit the displaced persons camps in order to recruit the various nationals to return to their home country. This meant that I, as the resettlement and repatriation officer, had to invite the Russian liaison officer to talk to the Estonian, Latvian, and Lithuanian nationals and try to "entice" them into returning to their respective countries. Many of those nationals did not want to go home and were leery of being exposed to a Russian officer. They were afraid that their relatives back home would suffer and perhaps be persecuted because of their unwillingness to return. The DPs feared that the liaison officer would bring with him some KGB people who would take photos of them with which to blackmail their relatives. Therefore, we went through the motions of having the Russian officer deliver talks to the displaced persons but always in my presence. The meetings were sparsely attended. At first I thought the reaction of the displaced persons was paranoid, but on further questioning, I came to the conclusion that their reactions were well founded in reality.

Another of my tasks was to help the military personnel organize spot-check inquiries in the camps in order to ascertain the camp population. The military representatives were under the impression that in order to receive adequate food supplies, some of the camps inflated their population numbers. This was undoubtedly the case, but in reality the amount of food requested was necessary for the displaced persons to survive. The camps visited for a spot check were populated mainly by adult Jews who were too smart to reveal their true population since doing so would result in a reduction of their food allowance. Although I was aware of what was going on, I did not give them away for obvious reasons. In reality, the Red Cross parcels did not contain any fresh food, and some of the dehydrated food was used to barter for fresh food in the German sector, something that was not officially allowed.

Since my job no longer included the personal touches I had relished, I decided that it was time for me to face up to life again as a civilian. I felt that I was something of a bird in a gilded cage, supplied with all the amenities, and might have a hard time adjusting to everyday life.

Although the job itself was quite demanding, I had no responsibility for taking care of my everyday needs. My food was served to me, I had a chauffeur, my clothes were washed and pressed, and the maid service cleaned my quarters. My salary, equivalent to that of a British judge, was paid in American dollars and converted into British pounds which were sent to my bank in London. Since I received a small allowance to take care of my daily expenses, I had saved a considerable amount of money and would not be financially stranded once I returned to Great Britain. Many of my colleagues wanted me to stay and thought I was "mad" to want to return to everyday life.

I had become well-adjusted to the "American ways" and found the mores of the US troops very pleasing. I found the Americans I was in touch with to be relaxed and easy-going, patient and companionable. Most of them were generous, open in their intentions, and somewhat naïve compared to the Europeans and far less inhibited in their wheelings and dealings. Certainly the Army was a select group of Americans, and I had experienced only a part of the US, but the average GI was far less stiff and repressed than his British counterpart. If he was displeased, he showed his displeasure openly. I liked this and could easily imagine living happily in the United States some day. I handed in my official resignation, having served more than three years, two more than I had promised. I received an honorable discharge and returned to London, which I considered to be my home.

The entire experience with UNRRA and the IRO had greatly broadened my horizons not only through all the friendships I had formed but also through all the suffering I had been exposed to. Still in my twenties, I had matured a great deal emotionally and intellectually. Although I was leaving all my friends, we vowed stay in touch, which many of us actually managed to do.

NOTES

1. Ora Markstein, telephone interview.
2. Marianne Guttmann Bolgar, *A Child Facing History*, unpublished memoir. Permission granted by Tibor Bolgar.
3. Three interesting books that deal with the impact of the Holocaust on survivors are *Children of the Holocaust* by Helen Epstein, *The Rage to Live: The International D.P. Children's Center Kloster Indersdorf, 1945-1946* by Anna Andlauer, and *Open Your Hearts: The Story of the Jewish War Orphans in Canada* by Fraidie Martz. All three books back up my contention that the vast majority of the survivors went on to live productive lives.

Chapter Eight

Back in London

Once back in London, I looked for a more comfortable flat and was able to rent one in my favorite part of London, Knightsbridge. My new apartment was on Pont Street, in the stately four-story house said to have once been occupied by Lady Hamilton. I occupied part of the second floor next to an apartment inhabited by a Lady and Lord. On the third floor were the living quarters and studio of Victor Cardew, an artist who taught at a prominent art school whose name I don't remember. Entering the spacious hall, one was greeted by a great hand-carved wooden table. The ground floor had a large ballroom. Elegant parquet floors graced not only the ballroom but all the apartments as well.

My flat, which had once been the library, was the smallest. A long hall led past the kitchen to a large octagonal room which had an impressive fireplace with a gas heater. From one corner of the room a passage led to the bathroom, which had an oversized bathtub with fancy feet with claws. Even the passageway was elegant, with indirect lighting, a milk-glass ceiling, and bookshelves lining the walls.

The building manager owned an antique store in Chelsea, and with my recently acquired financial security, I proceeded to buy a number of items from him including original paintings, Italian mirrors, two large Bukhara carpets, one in pink and one in dark red, and two large Louis the Fourteenth easy chairs with cerise silk backs and seats and elaborately carved wooden arms and legs covered with gold leaf. I also bought a gold-plated footstool, which is still in my possession to this day. My bed, which served as a couch by day, fit well into the niche of the room. But my most prized possession was a black lacquered French upright piano. I was looking forward to accompanying an old friend who played the flute. Together we played Bach, Mozart, Haydn, and Boccherini, reminiscent of good times back home in Vienna.

The building manager introduced me to the other tenants, who were polite and cordial, though the Lord and Lady were reserved and kept their distance. The Lord of Pont Street, as we called him, owned a large estate in Scotland managed by several of his employees, and he was bored in London, not quite knowing how to spend all his free time together with his wife, the Lady. It was painful to observe the limited horizons of those two. There was so much they could have done. I suppose they lacked the inner resources to occupy themselves in a productive manner. Soon I became friendly with the artist, who introduced me to a number of his friends. He entertained a great deal and his friends included not only artists but lawyers and other professionals, a bright and stimulating group.

In London one could rent a horse from a livery stable and ride along "Rotten Row" in Hyde Park. This broad track was originally called the Route du Roi (the king's road) but over the years it became "Rotten Row" because the Rotten Rich Victorians used to ride there in their Sunday finery to see and be seen. On weekends I rented a magnificent white horse named Napoleon and rode along this famous path. After all the years of struggle and hard work, I was beginning to feel like a member of the *haute bourgeoisie* once again. As I rode along, I looked at the well-dressed people riding towards me, half hoping to see Lady Norton who would be shocked by the improvement in my social class.

Once my flat was furnished, I began to look for employment. Kit Stewart from the London School of Economics recommended me to Betty Reed, the head social worker at the old and highly respected St. Thomas Hospital, where Florence Nightingale had worked, and the most desirable place for nurses to undergo their training. After the war child guidance centers in London were filled to their capacity, which motivated Betty Reed to look for someone to open a new therapeutic play center for the emotionally, physically, and psychologically deprived children in Lambeth. She offered me the job of Director, which I gladly accepted. The position entailed doing occupational therapy in the children's wards of the hospital in the mornings and running the Lambeth Children's Cottage after school. I was assigned the medical children's ward and had an assistant who worked in the surgical children's ward. The two of us played therapeutic games with the children and encouraged them to draw and model in clay. We sang songs with them and in general tried to create a therapeutic environment. When the weather was not inclement, we wheeled the beds onto the veranda so that everyone could enjoy the fresh air.

I found this assignment most gratifying—enabling the children to forget for a time the misery of their illness and the loneliness of being separated from their family. The hardest part of this job was to see young children dying.

THE LAMBETH CHILDREN'S COTTAGE

London is known for an abundance of capable volunteers who are eager to work in any capacity. As a result, I was blessed with a number of very capable volunteers, as well as an assistant, to help me with my work in the afternoon.

The Lambeth Children's Cottage, supported by the Northcote Trust, was a house built exclusively for children. It was located in a poor working-class district on the other side of the Thames, which in those days mostly consisted of slums. The cottage was located away from the street, with a paved yard where games were played. The two-story house had low ceilings and furniture the right size for children. On the ground floor there was a well-equipped kitchen. We had a catering license which enabled us to obtain the food we needed in spite of the strict rationing still in effect. On the ground floor there was also a large room used mostly by the boys, who built things from wood, hammering away. A short staircase led up to the second floor where there were three large rooms—an arts and crafts room, a game room, and a room we called "the dress-up room," which had a small stage.

When the children appeared after school, they were given the responsibility of purchasing and preparing sandwiches and a drink. We pointed out to them that if there was any money missing in the process of preparing their food, they were stealing it from themselves. Our budget was small so the children had to contribute a small amount towards what was often their only well-balanced meal of the day. In this neighborhood a mother might put out a loaf of bread and a stick of margarine and expect the children to feed themselves. Another common practice was to give the children a few pennies to buy chips at the local fish and chips shop. Visiting some of the children's homes, I witnessed such phenomena with my own eyes. As far as I could ascertain, very few of the parents were gainfully employed. Most of the fathers, who were unskilled laborers, were out of work. The mothers, if they worked at all, were mainly charwomen, working in factories and other industrial compounds.

The children were most creative in their drawings and their modeling with clay. Singing and acting were two of the most popular activities in the club, and the children were eager to dress up and put on plays. They rehearsed the plays just before the performance started, with all the other children rushing in to observe. The main theme of the plays reflected their family situations, such as a father coming home drunk and beating up the mother and/or children. This acting provided them with some relief and at the same time represented a cry for help. Another kind of help the children needed was medical. From time to time a nurse arrived to take them to delousing stations and examine them for contagious skin diseases such as impetigo.

Although the cottage had the capacity to handle forty children, there were only about twenty-five in attendance most of the time. Some children left early while others came later and had a hard time leaving. The children's ages ranged from eight to fourteen, and the majority were girls. On occasion they would bring younger brothers or sisters because there was no one to take care of them at home.

Stealing was the norm in this community, and the children had nimble fingers. They frequently stole money from the volunteers, no matter how carefully the volunteers hid their purses. The only person they did not steal from was me. They regarded me as one of them, which I considered to be a great compliment. Many of the children had been trained to beg for money and pick pockets on the streets and turn over their loot to their parents. They were also expected to pick up cigarette butts in the gutter so that the father could use the discarded tobacco to roll his own cigarettes.

When the children arrived at the cottage, they were dirty and unkempt, but with rosy cheeks. They loved to scrub themselves clean in the club's bathroom, probably because they had neither tub nor shower at their unhygienic homes. Many of the children showed me large holes in their socks. Others had no socks, wearing their shoes on bare feet even in winter.

We had very few rules at the club. One was not to steal food. A second was not to damage the toys and games. We explained that the toys and games were theirs to use and if there was damage, they would be the losers. The third rule was to clean the club each day before they left, so that they could come back to an orderly environment the next day. The external order requested of the children was meant to impose some internal controls upon them. It was interesting to note that there was one volunteer for whom the children refused to clean up. When I discussed this with her, she admitted that she did not believe the children should have to keep the club in order. She never articulated this belief to the children, but they sensed it.

The children were the salt of the earth—charming and somewhat naïve, in spite of having been thrust into adult behavior. They loved the club and came regularly. This was a place where they could be children. They could play to their heart's content and grow emotionally in the process. Play, for children, is a preparation for life, and their parents had not given them the opportunity to play. Instead they forced the children to hustle to bring in money, which the adults mostly spent on alcohol.

Some of the children were Cockneys, and they taught me some of their rhyming slang, a language in code that policemen couldn't understand. When a policeman was approaching on the street, for example, they would say,

"Here comes a plate of meat," meaning *policeman's feet*. Then they might say, "Let's go up them apples and pears," meaning *Let's go up those stairs*— no doubt to escape from the policeman.

In the district of Lambeth there was hardly any greenery to be seen—no trees, no bushes, no grass. I decided to take the children on a field trip to one of the parks in the West End. They had never experienced a meadow before and were enthralled. They threw themselves on the ground, rolled in the grass, and eagerly smelled the fresh air. I was very touched by their behavior and I took them on field trips to the various parks as often as I could.

None of the parents, nor any other adult for that matter, ever visited the club during the time I was director. In order to convey the purpose of the club to the children's parents, I made some house calls. My explanations were well received, perhaps because of the great reputation of St. Thomas Hospital and all the services it rendered to this community. Nevertheless, that not one parent ever visited the club speaks volumes.

The theme song of the club, chosen by the children, was "You Are My Sunshine." They sang this song over and over again. It was a metaphor for their feeling about the club and its staff.

When I emigrated to the United States, I kept in touch with the children of the Lambeth Children's Cottage. At Christmastime I wrote asking them what they would like as a present. The majority asked me for a pair of socks. Others asked for a stick of gum.

TRAVELS IN GREAT BRITAIN

Shortly after arriving home from Germany, I traveled by myself to the Channel Islands for a vacation. I had become intrigued with the islands while billeted in Normandy where the German soldiers, invading from the Channel Islands, had decorated the hotel walls with those hideous-looking naked women.

The Channel Islands are located between England and France. To get there I had to board a small plane seating only three passengers. This was no easy trip, since the plane dropped, often dramatically, whenever it encountered an air pocket.

The three main Channel Islands are Guernsey, Jersey, and Sark. Sark, the smallest, was ruled by Sibyl Hathaway, a Lady who inherited the title of the Dame of Sark, had a seat in the House of Lords, and dealt bravely with the German soldiers who occupied the island during the war. The middle-sized island, Guernsey, is very lush. It is famous for its dairy products, thanks to its well-fed Guernsey cows. No cars are permitted on the island and transportation is conducted by horse and carriage only.

I stayed on Jersey, the largest and most beautiful island, whose Jersey cows and dairy products are well known all over Europe. In addition to milk and cheese, Jersey is famous for its crayfish, as large and succulent as lobsters. I loved the rolling, well-maintained meadows and the abundance of roses and other flowers. Most of all, I liked the picturesque and rugged coastline with the tide ebbing in and out in a predictable manner. Before they became British possessions, these islands belonged to France. The natives therefore developed a language all their own, with elements of Norse, French, and English.

The other trip I took, also by myself, was to Torquay in Devon, in the southernmost part of Great Britain, where the water sports events of the Summer Olympics were held in 1948. Torquay is a popular vacation spot, known as the British Riviera because of its mild weather. The streets are lined with palm trees and the earth is a vivid, natural red. I took trips out from Torquay to see the moors and Stonehenge and enjoyed a very relaxing vacation. Here, as in the Channel Islands, the sea and the coastline were great drawing points for me.

EMIGRATION TO THE UNITED STATES

Erwin Pollitt and I had been corresponding with each other for nine years—ever since he left Great Britain to emigrate to the United States. He invited me to come to the United States so that we could become reacquainted. After a year and a half in London, I agreed to visit him to ascertain whether we still had a lot in common. I was quite sure that we did, since all this time we had been exchanging our news and thoughts and wishes with each other. I therefore applied to the American Embassy for a visitor's visa.

The British government had notified me that I could become a British citizen, which I considered a great honor. They also informed me that if I went to the United States and later returned to Great Britain, I would have to wait six months before becoming a British citizen. In anticipation of traveling to the United States for a visit, I sublet my apartment.

My efforts to emigrate to the United States had a long and tortuous history. When I fled from Vienna as a teenager, my affidavit to enter the United States was transferred to London. The immigration quotas to America were oversubscribed, and I was aware that I would have to wait for quite some time before my name would come up. Before leaving for Germany with UNRRA, I went to the American Embassy and handed in my post office number, in case my name came up while I was in Germany. My APO number was 157, which was located in Frankfurt. Someone in the American Embassy mistook the number one for a seven and sent my records to APO 757 which was the American Embassy in Paris. Consequently when the

American Embassy in London sent me a letter telling me to pick up my emigration visa, the letter with its wrong APO number took six months to reach me. Requesting an emergency leave, I traveled to London to pick up my visa. When I arrived, I was informed that I was too late and had lost my turn. This was obviously their fault, not mine, but that made no difference to the bureaucrats for whom a rule is a rule no matter what. I returned to Germany, since I was deeply involved in my work there and not ready to emigrate in any case. When my friend Barbara Donald visited the US Embassy in London on her way home to the United States, she had discovered that they had two names for me—Gertrude Stein and Gertrude Steinova—and consequently two sets of records.

Two weeks before my scheduled departure for the United States I assumed that all was well with my visitor's visa, and when I was summoned to the US Embassy, I naïvely imagined that they had asked me there to pick up this document. This was not the case. The bureaucrat informed me that they could not issue me a visitor's visa because I had applied for an emigration visa, and anyone who had at any time applied for an emigration visa was not allowed to enter the United States on a visitor's visa. My plans were set. I had sublet my apartment and had purchased my ticket to travel to the United States on the *HMS Mauretania*.

When I am enraged, I become cold and quiet and my thought processes become acute. With well-concealed hostility, I recounted in full detail the mistakes the embassy had made on my behalf. I began with the number mix-up which led to the six-month delay which led to my losing my place in line. I went on to explain that I was one person, Gertrude Stein—not Gertrude Steinova, the Czech variation of my name. Nor was I Gertrude Stein the well-known writer, nor Frau von Stein the friend of Goethe. I asked them why they had waited until the last moment—only two weeks before my scheduled departure—to inform me that I was not allowed to enter the US on a visitor's visa. Last of all, I pointed out that I myself had processed a large number of Holocaust-victimized children to emigrate to the United States on a non-quota basis. If they could enter the United States, why couldn't I?

Apparently, my words made an impression, because, after some discussion which took place behind my back, it was agreed that I could travel to the United States on an emigration visa. To me, this was an admission of guilt on their part for the mixed-up mess that had occurred.

The two weeks I had before my departure was a difficult time for me. Since I was emigrating, not just visiting, the sub-letting arrangement was off. I found a Spanish diplomat to take over my lease. Time was racing, and I needed to sell my beautiful antique furniture. When I explained my plight to the Spanish diplomat, she offered to buy the furniture for a modest price. I had no choice but to accept her offer. As an emigrant, I was legally allowed to take some furniture with me, so I took some tokens of remembrance—the

Louis XIV footstool, a painting given to me by my neighbor, two Sheridan trays, and a Sheridan-framed mirror from the seventeenth century. The Spanish diplomat made a very good bargain when she purchased my furnished apartment for a song.

Selling my furniture and all the contents of my apartment represented a total break from all the things I cherished. Added to that, I was leaving my dear friends behind. A visitor's visa had a temporary connotation, but the emigration visa meant something else psychologically. To me, it meant that my move to the United States would be permanent. This is what I had hoped for ten years before, but now that I was finally able to go, I became quite upset, felt insecure, and questioned my motivation. What happened was that I had formed roots in Great Britain much deeper than I was consciously aware of. Leaving England to work with UNRRA was not the same at all because I knew that my stay in Germany would be temporary and that my true home was in Great Britain where, on the whole, I had lived a peaceful and satisfying life. I had a circle of good, loyal, honest, and supportive friends there, a substitute family who had formed deep bonds with me.

After much thought, I told myself that this move did not have to be permanent and that I could return to England, should I so decide, whatever visa I possessed. This helped my state of mind a great deal. Leaving England had reactivated in me the losses I experienced when leaving Vienna, since I had not been able to work through all those losses, especially the loss of my family. If one can ever work through such losses.

TRAVEL TO THE USA

It was November 1949 and I was crossing the ocean. The *HMS Mauretania* was a luxury pleasure liner of the Cunard Line. I had the choice of third class or second class and chose second, which was located right in the middle of the ship, and indeed I found that I had made the right decision. The passengers were very interesting, not stuffy, and they represented a cross-section of mankind, a mélange of different types of people. We all saw each other day in and day out, always seated at the same table, and therefore had a chance to get to know each other, if only superficially. This arrangement offered me temporary security. Exchanging experiences around the dinner table one evening, I discovered that one of the passengers knew my cousin, the doctor in chemistry who lived in New York. What a small world it is.

In the late fall the sea was often quite choppy due to the violent weather. On stormy days we could not enter the dance floor or take walks on the promenade deck because the ship, knocked around by the waves, sometimes listed what seemed to me about forty-five degrees. Special dishes with magnetic bottoms had to be provided on such occasions so that they would not roll off the table onto the floor. I remember quite clearly that I was often the only person in the dining room for meals. I especially enjoyed breakfast. While everyone else remained in their rooms due to seasickness, I feasted on eggs and bacon—two foods that were severely rationed in Great Britain during and after the war.

The entire voyage lasted about ten days and proved quite therapeutic for me. It gave me time to rest and pull my thoughts and feelings together and at the same time, to pamper myself. It also gave me time to think about Erwin and to wonder how he had changed since I'd last seen him.

In some ways Erwin represented my past. He had known my family after my father's death, and they regarded him highly. The fact that I had lost my entire family to the Nazi regime strengthened the bond between us. When he had proposed marriage to me in London, I had turned him down. Now, however, the prospect of renewing and intensifying our relationship was not just comforting to me but exciting as well.

Erwin was born in Czechoslovakia, in a town called Brno and therefore came under a different waiting list to obtain his US visa, a much shorter list than the one I was on for Vienna. When he arrived in Great Britain, he was unable to work because he did not possess a worker's permit. His earnings from Austria had been sent to him in London so he had some money to live on while he waited for his visa, which came in a relatively short period of time. He left Southampton in early December, 1941. During his journey across the ocean, Germany declared war on the United States and everyone became apprehensive, fearing German U-boat attacks. The refugees on the ship were mainly German and Austrian Jews, fleeing to freedom. The Dutch crew, regarding them as enemy aliens, became abusive and mistreated them badly. Fortunately the ship arrived in New York without incident, much to everyone's relief. New York was overrun with immigrants pouring in by ship from Europe. On the advice of a Jewish committee, Erwin decided to settle in Minnesota.

Erwin had studied mechanical engineering at the University of Vienna and had earned a degree that was highly valued in the United States. His first position was working for a printing firm in St. Paul, Minnesota. The owner took a liking to him and introduced him to his friends at his country club.

As the war progressed, Erwin wanted to offer his services to the war effort. He found a position at the Armour Research Foundation, a branch of the Illinois Institute of Technology, a university located in Chicago that specialized in the training of engineers and psychologists. The Armour Research Foundation was comprised of highly trained scientists who were able to solve advanced and difficult engineering problems. They had many contracts from large industrial companies, as well as contracts from the US military.

As I was traveling the ocean, I had a little currency with me, and the rest of my money was in the form of a check in English pounds. While we were at sea, the value of the English pound depreciated rapidly. The irony was that I had originally been remunerated in dollars but had converted the dollars into pounds. The money I had brought with me was worth only about half as much as it had been when I left. I was no longer wealthy.

When we arrived in New York Harbor, we were welcomed by the Statue of Liberty. The statue, a metaphor for the United States and all it stands for, had a great emotional effect on me. To me it meant freedom of speech, freedom of thought, freedom from intolerance, freedom from repression, and a fluid class structure. No longer was I a foreigner in a strange land. Although I had felt at home in Great Britain and had many friends there who wholeheartedly accepted me, I could not forget the initial treatment that was handed out to me, demeaning me when I was in a situation of great need. Once I arrived in the United States, I felt liberated from all the chains I had been dragging around. I felt that this country was truly the land of opportunity and that now I could concentrate on moving ahead unencumbered.

Erwin flew to New York to welcome me, and after all those years of staying in touch by letters only, we had quite an emotional reunion. We were both eager to get to know one another again and found it easy to pick up where we had left off. I knew that once again I would have to get used to a new way of life—a new culture, new mores, new attitudes, new behaviors, new mannerisms. But this time the adjustment promised to be much easier than before. I was familiar with American ways from my time in Germany. Also I was more mature, more sure of myself, and this time I had Erwin, who was already a US citizen, to encourage me.

While in New York, we visited the United Nations Building, which was most impressive. I had arranged to travel to Washington DC to meet UNRRA friends, a trip that was arranged with Erwin's knowledge, and he traveled along with me. Our first stop was at the home of Barbara Donald, the former director of Camp Aschau and assistant to Walter Lippmann. She lived in a beautiful three-story Georgian house in the prestigious and historical area of Georgetown. Next we visited Gertrude Richmond and Connie Clark, the former heads of the UNRRA Child Welfare Department in the US Zone in Germany. They all welcomed us with open arms, wining and dining us and showing us around the beautifully planned city. We even had time to take in a few avant-garde plays. It was good to observe Erwin and my friends enjoying each other's company. Although it was November, the weather was mild and there were autumn-flowering cherry trees miraculously blooming in profusion. To me this seemed another sign of welcome. My wandering days were over. I had come home.

Chapter Nine

Chicago

We traveled by air to our final destination, Chicago, where I planned to start a new life for myself. Chicago is a bustling town, a melting pot providing an opportunity to succeed socially, economically, and culturally for people from all over the country. It used to be said that if you can't make it in Chicago, you can't make it anywhere. Carl Sandburg called it "the city of the broad shoulders," which I interpreted to mean tolerant and accepting. Unfortunately this did not apply to the black population, many of whom lived in a ghetto-like area on the south side, much to my horror. In spite of this, the average Chicagoan is a friendly, helpful, courteous human being.

Chicago has utilized the lakefront more beautifully than any other city in the country as it hugs the southwest shore of Lake Michigan, in the shape of a pregnant sausage. The lake, one of the largest freshwater lakes in the world, looks like the sea, since water and sky meet at the horizon. Chicago's lakefront is one great park, with large grassy areas, beautiful sand beaches, harbors, and a well-landscaped road running close to the shore.

Chicago has a river as well as a lake. The Chicago River is part of a waterway that extends all the way to St. Louis. Every year for St. Patrick's Day, the employees of City Hall dye the river green. The river has a large number of picturesque drawbridges which allow for the passage of barges, tug boats, and pleasure craft going back and forth from Lake Michigan.

Erwin lived on the North Side near Sheridan Road in a large, spiffy one-room apartment with maid service. When I first arrived, I stayed in a room in a small hotel but soon moved to a cheaper room in order to prevent my diminishing bank account from being depleted even more rapidly. This room was in an apartment in the Edgewater area. It was clean and well kept except for the kitchen. My landlady, a German immigrant, loved to eat but hated to wash up afterwards and always left dirty dishes piled high in the sink. Unable to stand this lack of hygiene, I ended up being the dishwasher. Shades of the past.

Christmas was coming and I decided to find a temporary job. I started on elegant Michigan Avenue, going from store to store offering my services as a salesperson. Everyone who interviewed me listened patiently as I described my background only to shake their heads because of "no American experience." Was this all these people cared about? Was I being viewed as a "bloody foreigner" once again? Not allowing myself to become discouraged, I pushed ahead to slightly less elegant State Street. There I landed a job selling clothes in the children's department of a large department store called Mandel Brothers. I received only a salary while the rest of the sales staff was given both a salary and a commission. Perhaps because of my pronounced British accent, most of the customers wanted me to wait on them, much to the chagrin of the other sales personnel, who deeply resented me.

After Christmas I was transferred to the credit department and assigned the job of credit interviewer. It was up to me to figure out who was and who was not eligible to receive credit, not a particularly challenging task. A few months of this was enough, and I managed to obtain a more gratifying job as intake interviewer at Michael Reese Hospital, a huge, highly regarded private hospital, one of the first in the country to start a unit for prematurely born infants.

WEDDING BELLS

My relationship with Erwin flourished. We became closer and closer and decided after a year and a half to get married. We took our marriage vows before the justice of the peace at City Hall on Friday, January 13, 1952. Our wedding reception was at the Kungsholm, a Swedish restaurant lavishly furnished with red velvet and gold trim. The restaurant housed a puppet show presenting various popular operas within a small, opera-like auditorium. As one listened to the opera and watched the skillfully manipulated puppets, one could easily imagine being in a real opera house. Some of my newly made friends from the hospital attended the reception and everyone had a good time, especially the married couple. To celebrate our honeymoon, we stayed in an elegant hotel on the South Side. The hotel overlooked the lake, but unfortunately we were unable to see it, since the fog was too dense.

Before our wedding, Erwin and I had thoroughly discussed my desire to continue my education in addition to my work. In those days it was more or less expected that a wife would stay home and do the housework. My vision of what it meant to be a partner in a marriage was somewhat different. Erwin was in complete agreement with me. He too felt that there should be equal responsibilities within a marriage and was pleased to have chosen a wife with professional ambitions. Since his salary was enough to sustain both of us, his views on this subject were purely socially and psychologically motivated.

At the time of our wedding I was living in a furnished apartment in an ivy-covered house on the South Side one block north of the Midway. My landlords were a charming elderly British couple who loved to exchange memories with me about their native country. Erwin was still living in his one-room modern apartment on the North Side. We needed to find another place to live, which wasn't easy since there was no building going on during and soon after the war. Erwin worked at the Illinois Institute of Technology, on the near South Side not far from the slums. Thanks to the recommendation of one of his colleagues, we eventually managed to obtain an apartment in the South Shore area, only a few miles from Erwin's work.

This apartment was within walking distance of a beautiful beach and during the summer months we spent a lot of time swimming and seeking the sun. Since the apartment was spacious and occupied a whole floor, we called it a flat. We carefully carpeted and furnished the place mostly with modern furniture except for the dining room, which was more traditional, in the British style. We entertained many guests in this apartment, especially colleagues of Erwin's from the Armour Research Foundation. It was a cohesive group of compatible people, like an extended family.

IN PURSUIT OF A BA

I felt a strong desire to go back to school. This urge was to reappear at frequent intervals throughout my life. Why was I so highly motivated? My parents had valued education and had high expectations for me. I had internalized their expectations and made them my own. For me, this was a way of partially compensating for their loss. There was another reason as well. I had found my work with UNRRA and my work at the Lambeth Children's Cottage to be most gratifying. I wanted to build on those experiences, be done forever with menial jobs, and get into social work, the helping profession.

I applied at Roosevelt College, soon to become Roosevelt University, for a re-evaluation of the credits I had earned in Great Britain. At this time European education was looked down upon in the United States, at least in the Midwest. This attitude and my original reception on the job market were both signs of the isolationist movement that thrived in the Chicago area, thanks in part to the *Chicago Tribune* and Colonel McCormick, its owner and publisher. Roosevelt University, however, was known for its open-minded policies and its devotion to social justice. The school was founded in 1945 by Edward J. Sparling. He had resigned from his position as President of the Central YMCA College in Chicago because his board wanted him to report on the demographics of his student body, the first step, he feared, in establishing a quota system to limit the number of Jews, blacks, immigrants, and women who could attend. Students and faculty had followed Sparling and helped him establish the new college, named in honor of Franklin D. and Eleanor Roosevelt. Early board members included Marian Anderson, Pearl Buck, Ralph Bunche, Albert Schweitzer, and my friend Ludwig's father, Thomas Mann. This promised to be a school that lived up to my hopes and expectations.

I received some credit for my studies at the London School of Economics. After undergoing an individual IQ test and a general admittance test, I requested an interview with Dr. Otto Wirth, who spoke to me in German. He was a semanticist and, like Henry Higgins of *My Fair Lady,* could ascertain just by speaking with me which social class I came from and what type of schooling I had had. He gave me sixteen hours of credit for my German and told me I was speaking "Schriftdeutsch," which is the equivalent of the King's English. I was advised to take an interdepartmental major in the social sciences, which meant courses in psychology, sociology, anthropology, political science, and economics. Because of my extensive training in biology at the London School of Economics, I was allowed to take courses at the premed level in order to fulfill the biology requirement.

It was no easy task for me to work all day and take evening classes at Roosevelt, but I was able to manage it with support from my husband. During the summer months I took time off from work and went to school full time. Eleanor Roosevelt came to visit the school on several occasions and lectured to us. I found her to be dynamic, impressive, and highly knowledgeable—a charismatic woman.

Because of my pre-med courses, I was able to obtain a position as a medical technician in the cardiac clinic of Northwestern University Medical School where I was assigned to take and develop electrocardiograms. In those days these were done by filming the heart rate of a patient and developing the film. At the same time I worked with a physician doing research into radioisotopes and helped conduct research on patients suffering from essential hypertension, that is, high blood pressure without any apparent physical causes. Although no one asked me for my religious affiliation, the medical school had a quota limiting the number of Jewish students to four percent. I sometimes wondered if Colonel McCormick, a big contributor to the medical school, had a hand in this.

My attendance at Roosevelt University helped me become quickly acculturated to the United States. The school was known for its liberal views, misinterpreted by some as "pinkish" leanings. The faculty members, mostly graduates of the University of Chicago, were open-minded and so was the student body. Thanks to the lack of a quota system, my fellow classmates were a group of mature, highly motivated students from a great variety of ethnic backgrounds. After class we usually met at a local bar where we sipped non-alcoholic beverages and continued to discuss whatever we were currently learning in class. I found this to be a very stimulating environment and an excellent learning experience. Erwin and I became friendly with a number of the students and professors, and some of these friendships remain strong to the present day.

I graduated from Roosevelt in the summer of 1954 with a bachelor's degree in the social sciences. I was eighth in a graduating class of 280 students. Erwin was proud of me and I was proud of myself and wished my family could have been there to help us celebrate. Though I looked forward to a break from my studies, I enjoyed school and knew for certain that this was not the end of my education but the beginning.

ON BEING NATURALIZED

To become an American citizen, I had to undergo an examination. I prepared for this by taking a class in American History at Roosevelt. Arriving at the examination for citizenship, I felt confident and secure, but when the examiner found out that I was attending Roosevelt University, he turned against me. He openly expressed a bias against the university and started asking me the most difficult questions he could find, such as "Name all the Presidents backwards" and "How many wards are there in the city of Chicago?" In spite of this, I did somehow manage to pass the test and become a US citizen.

IN PURSUIT OF A MASTER'S DEGREE

In the fall of 1954 I was enrolled at the School of Social Service Administration at the University of Chicago, to obtain a Master's Degree in social work.

In 1908 the Social Gospel minister Graham Taylor founded the Chicago School of Civics and Philanthropy, a pioneering institution that addressed itself to practical social problems such as juvenile delinquency, truancy, vocational training, and housing. Trustees of the Chicago School, including Jane Addams and Julius Rosenwald, were reformers and philanthropists dedicated to social betterment. Brilliant women, all residents of Jane Addams' Hull House, held key positions in the Chicago School, including Edith Abbott, who earned a Ph. D. in Economics from the University of Chicago, Julia Lathrop, the head of the Children's Bureau under President Taft, and Sophonisba Breckinridge, the first woman to earn a Ph.D. in Political Science at the University of Chicago and the first woman to graduate from the U of C Law School. These women were instrumental in bringing about a merger between the Chicago School and the University of Chicago in 1920, thus forming the School of Social Service Administration or SSA, the first university-based graduate school of social work in the nation. Edith Abbott, who became the school's first dean, set out to make the SSA the best social work institution in the United States, and according to my advisor at Roosevelt, she succeeded.

Based on my grade point average at Roosevelt, I was offered a fifty percent scholarship. In those days professional social workers were highly sought after, especially graduates of the U of C, and many agencies offered scholarships, provided the student would promise to work for them for a minimum of one year after graduation. My scholarship came directly from the university and had no strings attached. However, I was expected to attend school full time because of the fieldwork requirement. This meant spending three days a week in class and two days a week working, under the close supervision of a faculty member, at a public welfare or private social agency.

Not aware of how demanding this program would be, I called Dr. Bruno Bettelheim to offer myself as a part-time childcare counselor at the Sarah Shankman Orthogenic School, his residential treatment institution for severely disturbed youngsters. At first Dr. Bettelheim was his charming self, very cordial. Since he too came from Vienna, he was interested in my education both there and in England, and he spent quite some time talking to me. He finally asked me whether I was married, to which I answered in the affirmative. Suddenly his voice changed. He said, "I do not accept married women," and hung up on me, leaving me puzzled and stunned. I later found out that he believed that married women would not be able to commit enough time and effort to the children in their care. In later years Bruno Bettelheim and I enjoyed a close collaborative relationship based on the severely disturbed children I referred to his institution and my treatment of their parents.

The academic and social learning at the School of Social Service Administration was for me a great growing experience both emotionally and intellectually. The classes were small, and free discussion was encouraged. The faculty, all of whom were caring, concerned, and tolerant, were outstanding practitioners in their field. Many were well renowned nationally and internationally for their research, their writings, and their pioneering work. The lectures were dynamic and stimulating and the general focus of the teaching was psychodynamic, taking into account the unconscious, the preconscious, the ego, and the superego in the developmental process. Although some of the students came from the United States, others came from such places as India, Laos, Japan, Holland, Switzerland, and France. As we compared and contrasted customs and ideas and gained new insights into humanity and its social and economic needs, we could feel new windows opening within ourselves. The intellectual and emotional investment required of the students was great in this program, and in my view, some life experience and a degree of maturity were required in order to get the most out of our training.

PRACTICAL EXPERIENCE

My first year of fieldwork at SSA was at the Chicago Welfare Department on Damen Avenue, a public agency serving a multitude of people with a wide variety of nationalities, ethnicities, ages, and needs. I was assigned a teen-aged unmarried mother just up from the South, an unemployed man whose wife had run off leaving him to raise the five kids, and a senile elderly woman who had hidden her money under her mattress and forgotten where it was. The girl lived on the north side of Chicago, the man lived on the south side, and the old lady lived on the west side. I was expected to visit all three people in one day because my other day at the agency was reserved for paper work. To reach my clients, I had to take public transportation and walk alone through tough neighborhoods, clutching the black folder that identified me as a public social worker. Most of the people in these neighborhoods realized I was there to help, but on several occasions groups of young boys and teenag-ers attacked me with baseball bats. My only defense was to ignore them and walk on. These days were anxiety provoking, to say the least. I have vivid memories of walking up dark, narrow staircases on the verge of collapse in order to reach my client's apartment.

In order to graduate from the first year to the second of this program, we had to pass a comprehensive examination that lasted a full day. The first part of the exam tested our casework skills. This meant analyzing the case of a person seeking our help. We had to write our diagnosis and treatment re-sponse, revealing our interview skills, our nonjudgmental attitudes, and our diagnostic and treatment skills. The other part of the exam tested our admin-istrative acumen and statistical knowledge. I remember that one of the ques-tions was "What kind of social programs would you organize should there be another Depression?" The ability to move on to the second year was also dependent on the maturity, emotional stability, and nonjudgmental attitudes of the student, as observed by the student's supervisor of casework and one other faculty member. In this way, a number of people who were misfits for the profession were screened out.

In the spring of our first year students had to decide, with the guidance of the faculty, which specialization we wanted to pursue. Since my experience and background were in child welfare, I decided to enter this field.

During the summer recess after my first year of residency, I decided to seek more practical experience and took a temporary assignment as a social worker at Cook County Hospital, which serves mostly the indigent. I was placed into the pathological OB ward, which provided me with a great deal of practical experience. The load of daily referrals was horrendous and I had to use my diagnostic skills to decide which of my clients needed to be helped first. Who should take precedence? The retarded teenaged girl who had been raped or the obese woman soon to give birth who didn't know she was pregnant?

At the conclusion of the second year we had to take a ten-minute oral examination on a subject chosen by a faculty committee. The subject assigned to me was community social work. Since I had had no courses on this topic, I was poorly prepared to reply to the questions thrown at me. Nevertheless, I somehow managed to pass. In the 1950s formality was the rule and a ridiculous requirement of the SSA was that the student being examined wear gloves. Unprepared in this regard, we passed one pair of gloves from one student to the next. All these tests were eventually abandoned. My educated guess is that too many capable students flunked out.

THE JEWISH CHILDREN'S BUREAU

My second year residency was with the Jewish Children's Bureau, one of many affiliates of the Jewish Federation of Metropolitan Chicago. The JF provided a supportive network for the Jewish Community from birth to old age, with a variety of functions. They also served Christians and other non-Jewish individuals. They were an outstanding, well-organized, and highly professional organization.

The JCB provided a variety of services for children, both Jewish and non-Jewish. They supervised foster-home care and adoptions, and they placed children who needed it in specialized treatment centers all over the country. They also ran residential treatment centers for emotionally disturbed children and worked with parents.

The JCB was considered to be one of the best child welfare agencies in the entire country. It was well endowed and employed not one but five prominent psychoanalysts as consultants: Dr. Adrian H. Vander Veer, the head of the Child Analysts at the Chicago Institute for Psychoanalysis, Ner Littner, MD, who directed the Child and Adolescent Psychotherapy program for social workers at the Institute and served as consultant to the Child Welfare Department of Greater Chicago, George Perkins, MD, renowned child analyst and consultant to the Sarah Shankman Orthogenic School, and Dr. Bruno Bettelheim, who was the director of the Sarah Shankman Orthogenic School and led a weekly in-service training program for the JCB staff. Dr. Pieter Devryer, a full-time employee of JCB, headed the residential program for severely disturbed children. JCB also had a self-contained unit complete with its own cook and psychoanalyst in the Chicago State Mental Hospital, to deal with the needs of psychotic children.

I was assigned a varied caseload, working with different departments to serve the needs of the children. Along with being individually supervised by a staff member at JCB, I attended excellent in-service training programs there once or twice a week that added to my treatment capabilities and diagnostic skills. In addition, there were regularly scheduled case and treatment reviews. Everyone working with a particular child attended these meetings—the childcare counselor, the social worker, the psychologist, the casework director, the art therapist, the consultant psychoanalyst, and the supervisor of the residential unit. After pooling their observations, the staff went on to evaluate the needs of each child and plan the therapeutic approach likely to be most helpful. I found this agency and what they stood for to be very exiting, and my professional growth was greatly enhanced by this experience.

During my second year at the U of C many of the teachers assigned papers to be written on a variety of subjects, in addition to the master's thesis that had to be finished by a deadline. It seemed to me that each professor felt that he or she was the only one whose papers were important. In other words, there were so many papers due at about the same time that frequently I had almost no time to sleep. Somehow I managed to write the papers and turn them in without being penalized for lateness.

There was another paper as well, my first professional paper, written while I was working at the Jewish Children's Bureau. It was about a case I had treated by working with the whole family. We had managed to keep the child at home instead of placing her in a treatment center. The paper, entitled "Work with Child and Parents Towards Interfamilial Adjustment," was written for the Child Welfare League of America. They accepted the paper and included it in an exhibit that was presented to child welfare agencies all over the country. Ultimately my paper became part of their permanent library in Washington, DC. This honor made me almost grateful to those professors at the U of C who had caused me to stay up all night frantically writing paper after paper all of which seemed to be due at about the same time.

At the end of the second year the casework director of the JCB asked me to remain as a permanent staff member. I was thrilled to have been given this opportunity and accepted the offer with great enthusiasm. The agency was known to hire only experienced social workers to their staff, so adding me as a relative newcomer was a deviation from the norm.

Erwin had continued to support me in my studies. He was most patient in the lack of demands he made on me, and his encouraging words helped me a great deal to get through my studies. I was honored to be put on the Dean's list when I graduated in 1956 with my master's degree in social work in the field of child welfare. Once again Erwin was proud of me, I was proud of myself, and I knew my family would have been proud of me if they had been there.

SOCIAL LIFE

Except when I was staying up most of the night to write papers, Erwin and I managed to have a good social life, entertaining and being entertained by friends and, like the good Europeans we were, attending a great many lectures, concerts, plays, and discussion groups, some of them right on campus. One of the theater groups was unique. They met near the campus in the back room of a tavern that played Mozart most of the time. The performers were young comedians, most with some connection to the U of C, who improvised and ad-libbed to their heart's content.

You may have guessed by now that these performances were the beginning of the Second City Players. Many actors rose to fame from this group and are world renowned today. The original group, called the Compass Players, included Barbara Harris, Mike Nichols, Elaine May, Severn Darden, Byrne Piven, Paul Sills, Shelley Berman, and many others. A skit usually began with a comic analysis of an item in the news and took off from there. Towards the end of a show the actors would solicit ideas from the audience and improvise. These performances were so hilarious that they soon had to move to new quarters to accommodate the large audience. This was a most creative, intelligent group of actors, and their ability to ad-lib was outstanding.

Today the group is on American television. Mike Nichols is a famous movie producer and many of the actors have played major roles in the American film industry, for example, the late Gilda Radner and John Belushi. Being trained by and having "graduated" from the Second City Group is a high recommendation for any actor these days, and I am proud to have seen so many of them at the beginning of their careers.

VACATION

Between graduation and the beginning of my full-time position on the staff at JCB, there was time for a much-needed break. Erwin and I had taken car trips to state parks in Illinois and Indiana and we had driven to Colorado to hike in the Rocky Mountains, an activity we both loved dearly. This time we had three whole weeks to spend and decided to go to Hawaii. We traveled to three islands—Oahu, the Big Island, and Kauai—and took in the usual tourist destinations such as Pearl Harbor, Honolulu, and Diamond Head. We also enjoyed walks during which we observed beautiful waterfalls, spectacular rock formations, and active volcanoes. Our time in Hawaii was a welcome respite from everyday life, and it occurred to me how fortunate I was to have a good education, a wonderful husband, and a new position at an agency which would enable me to do the work I loved—to treat children who were burdened with a variety of serious problems.

BACK TO JCB AS A FULL-TIME STAFF MEMBER

Most of the children referred to JCB were severely disturbed. They came from dysfunctional families where the parents, for whatever reason, were unable to take care of them. These abandoned, rejected, and emotionally volatile children were developmentally arrested; that is, they acted as if they were much younger than their chronological age. Especially revealing was the girls' concept of themselves. When they arrived for placement, many of them brought their favorite doll with them, a doll wearing no clothes. This was a metaphor for their feelings of barrenness, abandonment, and lack of hope for a better future. The problems they presented varied in intensity. There were children who suffered from eating disorders, sleep disorders, sleep walking, enuresis, and encopresis, to name a few.

Our task was to give these children adequate care by finding them an appropriate foster home or treatment center and by providing them with individual psychotherapy with a member of our staff. We tried to convey to the children that we accepted them just as they were, and the demands we made on them were minimal. We provided a certain amount of security and structure for them, to help them adjust to their new environment. To illustrate my points, I would like to cite examples of two children who have given me permission to write about them.

LINDA

A six-year-old girl whom I'll call Linda came from France with her mother, who had been invited to do an internship with a plastic surgeon at a local hospital. Linda had to be placed in a foster home because her mother had not made any provision for her. This was a very frightened and severely depressed little girl who slept with her clothes on and refused to change them. Her mother tongue was French and she refused to learn to speak English. Linda was assigned to me, partly because I could speak a little French and partly because of my past experience with young children. One of the touching things Linda confided in me was that she was like a snail who carried her house on her back and when she became frightened, she quickly retreated into her house.

I treated Linda and helped her emotionally to adjust to the tender loving care she received in her foster home. Her mother visited her on rare occasions.

JANE

A far more difficult case was a girl I'll call Jane, who was referred to us by her mother who could no longer tolerate her "acting out" behavior. The mother was unable to set any kind of limits on her daughter, nor could her husband, and the child at age six was in control of both parents instead of the other way around.

Jane entered my office wearing three scarves and three hats, thrusting her body and her arms in different directions. She opened and closed her hands in a rhythmic fashion while drooling saliva. Her motor coordination was poor and so was her manual dexterity. Her anxiety at meeting a stranger was understandably quite high. Soon she went down on all fours and pretended to be a dog, barking loudly and revealing herself as a very disturbed and troubled youngster.

Neither the mother nor the intake worker had informed me of Jane's many allergies, and when Jane picked up a bowl of M&Ms and shoveled them into her mouth, swaying her body from right to left to reassure herself, I did not intervene. She was quite a verbal child and told me that her mother had a mother who was very strict and that Jane's own mother needed some peace and quiet in the house since she was unable care for or control her own daughter, meaning herself.

Jane did not play with any of the toys in my office and gave the impression of being adult-like in a pathetic sort of way. When it was time to go, she refused to leave and had to be carried back to her mother in the waiting room. Her mother asked Jane what she had been eating and Jane replied, "Chocolate." This set off Mother, who put her hand to her mouth and breathed a sigh of deep disgust. Upon observing this, Jane broke out in a rash all over her body. Nowadays we no longer offer candy at random to our patients. Food is given within a therapy session only if it is judged to be therapeutic. After her first session Jane told her mother that she had knocked a hole in the floor of my office and had crept into it. This statement revealed that she had tried to form a relationship with me and that she felt comfortable and secure with me.

This was the beginning of treatment which entailed an extensive period of time. Prior to coming to the agency Jane had had many different diagnostic evaluations and was thought to be retarded and to suffer from possible brain damage. Neurological and psychological tests proved this diagnosis to be wrong. In my own diagnostic evaluation I found Jane to be a very bright child who had great hopes for herself. Tests and the consultant psychoanalyst's interview with Jane proved my evaluation to be correct. Borderline Personality Disorder was the final diagnosis.

In her therapy sessions Jane worked on her emotional deprivation and reenacted several developmental stages of her life in which she had been traumatized. Her feelings came out in full force. She screamed, cried, and made many noises, all of which I accepted and interpreted to her on a level she could comprehend. Her sessions were volatile and intense. At times after working with her, I was emotionally drained and felt like Annie Sullivan must have felt trying to set limits on Helen Keller.

Eventually, by mutual agreement, Jane was placed in a therapeutic treatment center. She attended a special school provided by the agency and did very well under close supervision. Later she received a BA in psychology, got married and divorced, worked for seventeen years in a state agency, and became an Evangelical Episcopalian. In the 1970s, when she read about Erwin's death in the paper, she called me on the telephone. I was very touched by this and happy to learn that she was able to live independently and had made a reasonably good life for herself.

The Jewish Children's Bureau was like an extended family. Everyone at the agency was greatly invested in their work and collaborated well with the other staff members. We met together socially on many occasions, and there was a great deal of cohesion amongst us. This included not only the professional staff, but also the non-professional staff such as the secretaries. Erwin and I gave a big party for the agency as did many others. For our party we translated a Viennese play by Johann Nestroy into English, assigned roles to each of our guests, and had a wonderful time. Although few of Nestroy's plays have been translated into English, Thornton Wilder used the plot and most of the characters from one of them for his play *The Matchmaker*, which later served as the basis for the musical *Hello, Dolly*. We attended many JCB parties where songs were composed and executed, all in a very creative manner.

DRUGS

In those days no medications were administered to the children at JCB with the exception of a mild tranquilizer prescribed on rare occasions. It was our opinion that prescribing medications for a severely disturbed child is like putting a band-aid on a boil. It masks the symptoms but does not treat the underlying cause. Our treatment at JCB focused on the underlying causes of the presenting symptomatology. This required a thorough history-taking process of the developmental stages of each individual child in the context of his or her family and included a dynamic diagnosis and treatment plan, with periodic reviews.

This approach, lasting over an extended period of time, had good results, and we were able to cure a great number of children. What I mean by a cure is that the client can function within the community and develop a sustainable life situation for himself. Many adults whom I treated as children have returned to visit me for a session or two and proudly tell me of the positive results of their treatment.

Drugs are inhibitors of pathology but they do not provide a cure. When a patient stops taking the drug, the symptomatology often returns with a vengeance, frequently in a more severe form. I have seen this over and over again in my practice, and it is regrettable that so many people are seeking the magical pill to take away all their symptoms without their having to take any responsibility themselves. The pharmaceutical companies encourage this delusion. Just take a look at their advertisements.

UNCLE FILIP

While working at the JCB, I was asked to place a disturbed boy into a treatment center in Rhode Island. This was not an easy task. Tired and exhausted, I was staying in a hotel room overnight before flying home to Chicago and I decided to call Arthur Brauch, my mother's cousin now living with his family in New York City. He was the cousin who had left Vienna with all his assets converted into jewelry, thanks to my uncle Filip. Although Arthur had never communicated with me, I felt that getting in touch with him was the right thing to do. At the same time, I hoped that he would have some information about my family.

He answered the phone and instead of expressing pleasure at hearing from me or asking me how I was, he uttered the following words in the most cruel and detached manner: "By the way, Filip was shot in the streets of Vienna because he could not bend up and down fast enough in an exercise given to him by a Nazi Storm Trooper."

This horrible news came as a huge shock to me. I was too stunned to ask any further questions. My feelings of guilt were reactivated and, irrational as it was, I blamed myself for not having arranged for my mother and aunt and uncle to leave Nazi Austria.

PRIVATE PRACTICE

While I was at JCB, a number of the consulting psychoanalysts started to refer private patients to me. Before I was allowed to take anyone on as a private client, the director of the agency had to give her approval.

There was a mother whose daughter was placed at the Menninger Clinic, a placement center and hospital for emotionally disturbed children. The child's original diagnosis was that of a hebephrenic, a severe mental disturbance. This child was cured and sent home to her mother. The JCB was no longer responsible for taking care of the child, since the agency took care of placed children only or, as in Jane's case, of children who badly needed to be placed. Since I was the mother's caseworker, it seemed prudent that I continue working with her rather than referring her to another agency. Mary Lawrence, the director at the time, approved of my taking the mother into my private practice. Although I saw Mrs. X at the same time and place, namely in my office at the agency, I was now carrying the sole responsibility for her as her therapist with no agency to back me up. This was to me a somewhat frightening experience and I had to use my analytic knowledge on myself to calm my anxiety.

ANALYSIS

As I became more educated and aware of the techniques and practice of psychotherapy, I also became more aware of my own inner feelings. Working with children, I found that their defenses are not that firmly established and they are more in touch with other people's feelings, be it their parents, their teachers, their friends, or their psychotherapist. The children I treated, most of whom had been rejected or abandoned by their family, reactivated within me losses of my own which I had partially repressed. In order not to over-identify with my clients and lose my objectivity, I realized that the time had come for me to enter into treatment and work on my depressive core. I therefore decided to undergo psychoanalysis. This required a commitment of time, energy, and money and, according to the rules, I had to pay the fee myself.

To undergo psychoanalysis turned out to be the right decision. It enabled me to clear out some of the "cobwebs" of my mind. My neurotic defenses were exchanged for healthier ones. Some of my repressions were lifted and resolved and I was able to function much better as a psychotherapist, a human being, and a member of society. My analysis lasted for five years on a three-times-a-week basis. My analyst, Dr. David Rest, was a very experienced, benign, and caring human being and we were well matched. I was able to identify with his inner security and he was amazingly in touch with all my feelings, psychological blocks, denials, and partial resistances, all of which he handled professionally very well.

While I was undergoing analysis, a letter telling more about the fate of my mother finally caught up with me. Twenty years before, in the middle of the war, Uncle Filip had written to my visa sponsor in Portland, Oregon, and the letter had traveled around the USA for several years before it reached me. My educated guess was that Uncle Filip did not want me to hear this terrible news by letter and felt that perhaps my sponsor could break it to me more gently. The letter described how brave my mother had been as she gathered a few of her belongings before leaving for Theresienstadt concentration camp, the camp the Nazis set up as a showcase to convince the Red Cross that the

Jews were treated well. Once again, my feelings of guilt were activated. Somehow I should have found a way to save them in spite of Mother's poor health, their massive denial, and their determination to stay in Vienna. My analyst helped me work through all these feelings. I never found out whether my mother was shipped off to a death camp. I hoped that her weak heart gave out before that happened.

At the end of the fifth year of my analysis, I felt healed. I was more secure and more tolerant, enabled to liberate and utilize a healthier equilibrium, with more energy and motivation to give to others and enjoy life. I was honored when my psychotherapist referred a distant relative of his to me for psycho-therapeutic intervention.

Erwin had been analyzed back in Vienna by one of Freud's disciples and was, on the whole, supportive of my analysis since he understood the process and knew how beneficial it could be. There were times, however, when he felt competitive with my analyst. It often happens that when one marriage partner is in analysis the other feels left out, isolated from the patient/analyst relationship.

THE INSTITUTE FOR PSYCHOANALYSIS

The title Psychotherapist was given to a few caseworkers at JCB who had proved themselves proficient in the psychotherapeutic treatment of children. Although I was blessed to be one of them, I felt that I needed more training and knowledge if I was to be worthy of my newly acquired title.

The Institute for Psychoanalysis was founded in 1932. The first Director was Franz Alexander, MD, who had his training in Europe and was of Hungarian origin. He initiated the psychoanalytic exploratory studies of psychosomatic diseases, an innovative focus which made the Chicago Institute well known all over the US and Europe. The next Director was Dr. Gerhard Piers, who came from Austria. He too was well known for his original thinking and for his book *Guilt and Shame*. When I became a student at the Institute, the faculty jokingly referred to it as the Austrian-Hungarian Empire.

The Institute offered a course originally called Child Care that was initiated by Dr. Irene Josselyn, a social worker who became an MD psychoanalyst. Originally analysis was not a prerequisite for taking the course, but when Dr. Ner Littner took over the directorship of the course, he changed the name to Child and Adolescent Psychotherapy, made its content more stringent, and required that those attending the course undergo a personal analysis. This requirement limited attendance by many mental health professionals, and it was mainly social workers who subscribed to the course.

The course I took entailed four years of part-time study plus two supervised control cases. This meant that I would be treating two children or adolescents for two years under the supervision of an analyst from the Institute. The course gave me a chance to meet and interact with other healthcare professionals and to see how people in other disciplines approached the psychotherapeutic process. Most important, it sharpened my diagnostic skills, my knowledge of child development, and my self-perception. I became more aware of my involvement in the psychodynamic treatment process, all of which was psychoanalytically oriented. When I completed the course, I was offered a position teaching this very course. I had to decline because I had just rented an office for my private practice and was unable to change it to the required day. Several years later I did teach a course for social workers at the Institute.

WORKING FOR THE PROFESSION

Work at the JCB went on uninterrupted and I slowly built up my private practice and became active in several professional organizations, setting and enforcing ethical standards for the profession, negotiating for pay increases and retirement benefits for all the employees at the JCB, and working toward the licensing of social workers.

In the late 1950s there were only a handful of social workers in private practice, though a few had some private clients in addition to working within an agency. I undertook a research study amongst social workers with some clinical knowledge and training to determine whether they thought their colleagues or they themselves were ready to enter private practice. The study revealed that the vast majority of those interviewed were in favor of having clinically trained social workers open their own private practice. This study was published in the professional journal of the NASW (National Association of Social Workers). Equivalent studies undertaken in other states at about the same time reached the same conclusion. To me this meant that the profession had matured and was ready to move ahead.

Somehow I felt that I was a pioneer in the development of the private practice of social work. Although very few people undertook this venture at that time, I started my own private practice on a full-time basis. My analysis helped me to stand on my own two feet professionally so that I felt secure enough to do this. It seemed like a good idea, especially after Erwin and I decided to move to the Village of Glencoe, a northern suburb of Chicago.

VACATIONS

While living in Chicago, Erwin and I had a favorite vacation spot that we returned to several times—Rocky Mountain National Park in Colorado. We both loved hiking in the mountains, and the Rockies reminded us of the Alps.

On one occasion we hiked up Lookout Mountain near Golden, Colorado. Well beyond timberline, we found a fire tower manned by college students This must have been a lonely job, for they seemed delighted to socialize with us and hear news of the outside world. To us it was exhilarating to climb so high and view the expansive valleys and rugged snow-capped peaks stretching out in all directions. It gave us the feeling that we had conquered nature.

When we first arrived in Estes Park, it was after dark and we stopped at the only motel we could find with a vacancy sign. As the motel owner started to hand us our key, she stopped abruptly and inquired with an edge to her voice, "You're not *Jewish* by any chance, are you?" Erwin and I were speechless. This was the first time we had encountered ant-Semitism in the USA, this country that had been so welcoming and had made us feel accepted and secure and had given us a place to live and work and thrive. We were about to leave to sleep in our car, but for some reason the woman suddenly felt sorry for us and allowed us to stay. We stayed there for an entire week. As the motel owner became more familiar with us, she decided she liked us and uttered, "You are not like the Denver Jews." This woman wrote to us every Christmas after that, trying to make up for her prejudice. I always wrote back, hoping that she would stop and think before turning away one of those Denver Jews she so despised.

During another Rocky Mountain vacation Erwin and I, along with a number of JCB employees, sojourned at a ranch resort that was eight thousand feet above sea level. The Aspen Lodge was a special place. It was owned by a former Austrian national, and the food was outstanding. One day we rode on horseback high up into the mountains. The horses were well trained to climb up the steep rocky paths and refused to budge when we misdirected them. But when it started to thunder and rain, the horses decided to go home, regardless of our wishes. They galloped uncontrolled through bushes and trees with no regard for their passengers. We clung for dear life to the horns of the Western saddles and ducked down as low as we could to keep from being swept off by the low hanging branches that whipped across our faces and shoulders.

In our effort to become well acquainted with our adopted country, Erwin and I traveled all the way to the Pacific Ocean. We flew to San Francisco where we visited friends of Erwin who showed us around this very beautiful, European-type town. We rented a car and drove south on Highway 1, spending a few days each in Monterey, Carmel, and Santa Barbara and ending our journey in Los Angeles where we had a wonderful visit with Erwin's aunt, her husband, and their son with whom I am still in touch to this day. It was heart-warming for me to have some relatives on my husband's side. Erwin's parents had both passed away before the war and I had yet to find any of my own relatives in the USA. Erwin's relatives, who were most hospitable, showed us many of the interesting sights around Los Angeles and Hollywood, including the filming of a scene from the Perry Mason Show in which a friend of Erwin's played a part.

The next trip we took was along the east coast. We drove to Portland, Maine, and traveled south along the rugged coastline. We always tried to do some research before venturing out on a trip. During the Depression unemployed writers, sponsored by the WPA (Works Project Administration), wrote travel guides that described in detail the many beautiful, quaint, historical, and interesting sights in the USA. These books never went out of date and we found them most useful in planning where to go. We traveled south from Portland to Kennebunk Beach and from there to Boston, ending our trip on Cape Cod, which we liked very much. From that day on we visited the Cape every summer. We enjoyed the cultural activities we found there, with all the off-Broadway theater companies and concerts to be found in different towns and villages. The quaint antique stores and the friendly, cultured residents all made a deep impression on us. As always, I enjoyed the nautical atmosphere and being close to the sea.

Chapter Ten

Glencoe

During my work at the Jewish Children's Bureau, Erwin continued his assignments at the Armour Research Foundation. While there, he created seventeen inventions having to do with color printing processes and printing machines. Erwin wrote his own patents regarding his inventions, which were of great benefit to his profession, and over the years he received many acknowledgments, especially from colleagues in Europe.

In the early 1960s there was a disagreement between the Illinois Institute of Technology and the Armour Research Foundation which I was not privy to. I do know that the Armour Research Foundation, through their exceptional work assignments, produced a great deal of money, a significant part of which went to support IIT. The outcome of this disagreement was that most of the important scientists from the Armour Research Foundation first revolted and then resigned. Erwin was one of the scientists who left their organization in disarray.

With his background and experience, he had no trouble finding another position and accepted an appointment in the research and development department of a food company located in Barrington, a distant northwestern suburb of Chicago and a fifty-mile drive from our flat in South Shore. Under these circumstances we were forced to leave South Shore, the cohesive community where we had formed roots, and move to the northern suburbs of Chicago.

Our friends and neighbors thought us to be "finks," deserters from the community. We had no choice, however, so we spent every weekend house hunting, a somewhat unwelcome and time-consuming task. Our real estate agent was a pressured and very hyper individual who dragged us to so many houses that it was difficult to sort them all out in our minds. However, the American dream to own a house was a dream with which we identified, and we finally found the house for us —a newly built three-bedroom, two-bath-room, prairie-style bi-level house in the Hubbard Woods section of Glencoe.

It was heart wrenching to have to sever our good relationship with the South Side community. To make matters worse, I was leaving the JCB and several close friends there to go into private practice full time. The many moves and separations Erwin and I had both undergone in our lives always made it hard to work through a new separation, even though this one was an improvement in our standard of living and we would be close enough to former friends and neighbors not to lose touch completely.

Our decision turned out to be a good one, in part because of the reduced distance Erwin had to travel, and also because Glencoe, a village of 11,000 inhabitants, was another cohesive and well organized community filled with interesting, friendly people.

NEW HOUSE, NEW NEIGHBORS

Our moving day took place in November during a snowstorm. We had to stop at a hardware store to purchase shovels in order to shovel our way into our house. The next morning a welcoming committee in the form of a dele-gated neighbor arrived, handing us a home-baked pie. This was an estab-lished custom. In this neighborhood people helped each other out by lending each other tools, offering advice, watching each other's children, and taking care of each other's pets during vacation time. The many little friendly acts we encountered gave Erwin and me the feeling that the neighbors genuinely cared about each other.

Block parties were held three times a year, usually in someone's home. Everyone brought something, perhaps some chairs for a breakfast party or something sweet for the Christmas party. In summer we had an outdoor block party coordinated by a committee of neighbors which changed every year. Everyone participated by contributing food. The police, who also repre-sented the fire department, would bring their fire engine to show off to the children, and special games were conducted for the children. Everyone en-joyed themselves and people who might not otherwise have known each other found things in common and became friends.

The houses on our street were a mélange of different architectural styles, and the gardens revealed a beautiful variety of flowers and designs. The street was lined with huge oak trees dating from the time when the area was virgin woods. The trees kept the area cool and pleasant, even on hot summer days. An array of professional and business people of different ethnic, relig-ious, social, and economic backgrounds populated the neighborhood. Erwin and I seemed to fit in well and befriended a number of people.

Amongst any group of neighbors, there are always a few who stand out. Opposite our house lived a young couple with three children. The mother was called "The Pied Piper of Glencoe," based on her willingness to entertain neighborhood children in her backyard. There were always a few parents to watch the children while others left to do errands. It was a well-supervised playtime for the children, who enjoyed each other's company and had an excellent educational experience.

Another unusual neighbor lived two houses south of us. He built a helicopter in his basement which he showed off to all of us with pride and joy. The only problem was that the helicopter was too large to be moved from his basement. When he and his wife eventually moved away, he had to dismantle the helicopter in order to take it with him.

Several houses to the west of us lived an elderly lady, a widow who kept a huge boa constrictor in her basement which consumed a chicken a day. The neighbors worried. What if the snake escaped? Boa constrictors, though non-venomous, coil around their prey and kill them by suffocation. A number of neighbors complained to city hall and the lady was asked to donate this animal to the zoo, which she eventually did.

Since our new house sat on a half-acre lot with no landscaping, we had to start from scratch to enhance the looks of the property. Because of the high cost of this venture, we employed a landscape architect who was willing to add trees and bushes and groundcover one section at a time. Three years later the landscaping was complete, and it was a beautiful sight to see. There were evergreen bushes planted in front, as well as an ornamental Japanese lilac tree whose blossoms gave out a very pleasing fragrance. From early spring to late fall there was always something in bloom. A star-magnolia was one of the first bushes to bloom in the spring, and a witch-hazel tree bloomed in October. The Japanese maple trees and the large, specially trimmed crab-apple tree gave the yard a somewhat Oriental look. We also planted two large rose beds, which I tended. Although Erwin and I both enjoyed working in the yard, it eventually became too much for us and we employed a yard service to help with the heavy work while I continued to take care of the roses and other flowers. Digging into the ground and reaping the results of one's labor is very gratifying emotionally and physically. My interest in yard work was partly due to my identification with my father and the love of nature which he implanted in me.

PRIVATE PRACTICE IN GLENCOE

My private practice thrived as I became more recognized as a psychotherapist within the community. When we moved to Glencoe in 1963, there were only three full-time private practitioners on the North Shore. All three of us were clinical social workers, all three had our training through the Jewish Children's Bureau, and all three specialized in the treatment of children. In those days, when private practice of social workers was just starting to develop, there were not enough rules and regulations. There was, however, a Private Practice Committee formed under the aegis of the National Association of Social Workers which organized a panel of experienced and highly respected social workers to interview prospective private practitioners and decide whether they were ready to undertake this venture. This committee was well organized and professional and their requirements for admission to practice were reasonable and ethical.

Grammar schools and high schools in the various suburbs started to refer children and their parents to me, and I became the consultant to the North Shore Congregation Israel Nursery School and the Winnetka Community Nursery School. A three-year-old boy whom we shall call Joe was referred to me, with the parents' written permission, by the Winnetka school for a diagnostic evaluation.

I observed Joe at the nursery. He sat on the floor in a corner leaning against the wall, neither smiling nor talking but observing all the happenings around him. Any attempt at involving him in activity was without avail. Nor would he go to the toilet. To my surprise, Joe was relaxed when he came to see me at my office. He became engaged with the toys, focusing his attention on the doll house and the family of dolls. He revealed good motor control and manual dexterity and soon showed himself to be an intelligent child who related easily and age-appropriately to me. He re-enacted his behavior at the nursery by picking a young boy doll who, like him, sat on the floor and did not participate. At the same time the doll representing his four-year-old sister was at home with the mother doll, having a fine time and receiving tender loving care. Clearly Joe was jealous. Using words he could understand, I explained to him that at the nursery school he was immobilized by his thoughts, wondering what his sister was doing at home with his mother. I pointed out to him that even though his sister had their mother all to herself in the mornings, he had his mother all to himself in the afternoons while his sister was attending nursery school. This was a revelation to him, a fact he had not considered. He let out a great laugh of relief, clapped his hands, and smiled. From that day on he participated happily in all the activities the nursery school had to offer, including visiting the toilet.

The school social workers took me under their wings and I was asked to their conventions to give papers which they published in their journals. Social workers' fees were lower than those of psychiatrists and psychoanalysts. We therefore met the needs of families in the lower income group. Nevertheless, I did see a number of people from affluent families who felt the need to seek psychotherapeutic intervention.

At first I rented an office in the middle of Glencoe. As my practice grew, I made the third bedroom in our house into an office. The house had a separate entrance which provided privacy for my clients, who could enter and leave the premises without being seen by the next client.

While exclusively in private practice, I felt a need to be in contact with other mental health professionals. I therefore organized a study group. There were about ten of us—secure and seasoned clinicians who brought to the meetings our concerns about our treatment of different clients. We sought help in refining our diagnostic evaluations and treatment skills and in dealing with the feelings our clients reactivated within ourselves. We became a tightly knit group, with Dr. George Perkins, a well-known psychoanalyst, at the helm. Dr. Perkins was very astute, accepting our blind spots and gently guiding us to improve our treatment and diagnostic skills. His particular knowledge was in the treatment of severely disturbed children, adolescents, and adults. Needless to say, we observed the confidentiality of all our clients to the letter, since all cases presented were well disguised.

After a few years Dr. Perkins fell ill and was unable to continue. I decided to organize my own study group conducted in my own home. Instead of ten practitioners, I recruited five or six. I felt that in a smaller group each person would gain more individual attention and have a deeper learning experience. This group went on consistently and well attended for thirteen years.

Among the many children I treated in my private practice in Glencoe, there were John, Susan, and Mark, whose names and circumstances I have changed to preserve confidentiality.

JOHN

John was a young teenager referred to me by the juvenile court because he was found loitering on the streets during school hours in an inebriated state. His mother would drive John to school and watch him enter. Once inside the school, he would immediately exit out a back door and join his pals of the same orientation. This pattern had started at the beginning of his freshman year.

John, the youngest of three children, was assigned the role of the black sheep in the family, rejected by both parents as well as by his siblings. He was often locked out of his own home and forced to sleep in the bushes. John's school phobia started when his parents had separated.

I treated this acting-out and dejected youngster for two years. On several occasions he mutilated himself, burning his flesh with a cigarette. One of the reasons he did this was to encourage his parents to take care of him. To me he said, "I do it because it makes me feel alive."

It became apparent to me that if John was to get well, he needed to be removed from the family that did not want him. I found a specialized out-of-state residential treatment center which his aunt agreed to finance, since his parents were not willing to do so. John received intensive psychotherapy at the center. He was closely supervised and his self-mutilation stopped. The treatment there, building on the two years he spent in treatment with me, proved successful, and John was able to complete his education, get married, and lead a productive life.

SUSAN

Susan, at age six, was a sad and depressed little girl who spent most of the day just moping around. Her parents had adopted her when she was an infant but instead of enjoying their daughter, they went through a mourning period. Both parents were infertile and their adoption of Susan reinforced their feelings of insecurity and inferiority. These parents had no inkling of the right way to tell Susan that she was adopted. The birth mother of Susan's imagination resembled the old woman who lived in a shoe. In Susan's therapy sessions with me, she re-enacted her fantasy of what had happened, which went something like this:

> There was an old woman who lived in a shoe.
> She had so many children she didn't know what to do.
> She gave them some soup without any bread
> And spanked them all soundly and sent them to bed—
> Except for me. I was the naughtiest, so she kicked me out of the shoe.

I helped Susan come to terms with her feelings of rejection by the birth mother, and I worked with the parents to help them handle their problems concerning adoption and to explain the adoption to Susan in an appropriate way. Susan gained a great deal from her therapy and became an active and alert youngster. The parents, on the other hand, remained sad and depressed, unable to fully accept Susan as their daughter.

Not long ago Susan called me from her home in California. She informed me that she is doing well and is happy, with a husband, children, and a good job. She thanked me for my warmth and understanding and for the support I gave her when she was a child. She said that her therapy was one of the happiest times in her childhood.

MARK

Mark at age six was severely depressed. In school he sat in a corner and did not respond to the teacher's requests. He would walk to school in winter without a coat because he wanted everyone to know that his mother did not take adequate care of him. Mark's mother slept late and prepared neither breakfast nor lunch for her very needy son. At night he walked in his sleep and always woke up by the refrigerator, thus revealing his oral deprivation. Both parents were rather cold and detached personalities who themselves had undergone early deprivations similar to those re-enacted by their son.

I treated Mark, in part through play therapy, for a number of years, helping him to overcome his depression and some of his needs by my caring and empathetic attitude, interpreting his frustrations in a language he could comprehend. I treated his parents as well, and after about three years of intensive treatment, Mark's acting-out and depression subsided and consequently he was able to sit in his regular seat at school and start learning.

Years later, Mark came to see me. A good-looking and well-developed young man, he had become a Protestant minister. From his six-foot-tall vantage point, he looked down on me and told me, "I remember you as very tall." He also remembered the play therapy we did together, and he thanked me for helping him overcome his inner sadness. I was quite touched by his visits and his vivid memories of the past.

GOOD YEARS

Although he liked his job in Barrington, Erwin decided to go into private practice. He became the consultant to a number of large companies such as Bell and Howell and the Sarah Lee food company. He felt secure and pleased with his decision to go out on his own and share his expertise with others.

Erwin and I had several good years while living in our house in Glencoe. We loved our work and each other, enjoyed our neighborhood, socialized with friends both new and old, regularly attended art exhibits, the symphony, the opera, and various theaters, one of which was the Writers Theatre, located in the back room of a book store in downtown Glencoe. We enjoyed winter vacations in Florida and summer vacations in Door County, a peninsula in Wisconsin that reminded us of Cape Cod, and eventually employed a travel agent to help us plan trips abroad.

FOREIGN TRAVEL

On our first trip abroad, we flew to Mexico. We took in most of the sights in Mexico City, Taxco, Acapulco, and Oaxaca, the town we liked best with its pyramids, bands playing in the town square, and Indians who take pride in their expert weaving and needle work. On our trip home we flew over Mexico's two magnificent snow-covered extinct volcanoes, Popocatépetl and Iztaccihuatl.

Our last trip abroad, in the early 1970s, was almost disastrous. We flew to Madrid, where I fell ill. The local doctor diagnosed my ailment as hepatitis, since my symptoms were vomiting and diarrhea. Although I did not feel good and needed extra sleep, we carried on with our plans, visiting the Prado and another art museum out of town. From Madrid we traveled to the island of Madeira, famous for its beaches, wine, fancy needlework, flowers, and flowering mimosa. Funchal, the capital city, is picturesque, with ox-drawn carriages and flower vendors who spread out their wares in the large court-yards paved with mosaics. The furniture in our hotel room was all made by hand, and our bed, covered with a European-style eiderdown, was so high off the floor that we had to use steps to climb into it.

Our final destination was the Canary Islands, located off the northwest coast of Africa. The islands, the Florida of Europe, were newly popular with American tourists, since Jacqueline Kennedy had visited there. People wrongly assume that the islands are so named because so many people keep a caged canary as a pet. Actually the islands were named by the Ancient Romans, who called the islands "Canariae Insulae" because there were so many large and ferocious wild dogs (*canes*) roaming about. So the birds were named for the island, not the other way around.

Erwin and I stayed in an elegant hotel on the Grand Canary island. The swimming pool was located on the roof, overlooking a vast expanse of beau-tiful beaches. At night the large dining hall was filled with people in evening gowns and tuxedos. Dinner was served Spanish-style at 8:00 PM, and we didn't eat, we dined, with a minimum of eight courses and the appropriate wine to accompany each course. The menu was written in four languages—Spanish, French, German, and English. Erwin and I had the feeling that we were living in another era.

Since I was still not feeling well, I consulted a British doctor who agreed with the other doctor that I had hepatitis. Assuming that I had a milder form of the disease, we continued our trip, exploring other islands and enjoying the beautiful beaches, the mountainous scenery, the ideal weather conditions, and the luxurious shops. Many natives of the region, who are Spanish or Portuguese, lived with their goats in caves in the mountains. Although the government built public housing for them, they preferred their caves and refused to leave them. Retirees of various nationalities have settled in the islands, and among them are many artists who can often be seen painting under the huge trees in the town squares. We ended our trip in Portugal where we explored Lisbon and its medieval quarters.

When we returned to Glencoe, my doctor informed me that I had been misdiagnosed. I did not have hepatitis but had suffered a massive heart attack—a coronary thrombosis. This should not have come as a surprise, since both my parents suffered from heart disease. I was instantly hospital-ized. By-pass surgery was not that well developed at the time and I was told that it was too late to perform surgery. To this day, I am amazed that I managed to survive the trip. It was our conclusion that I must have had a guardian angel watching over me.

My doctor told me that if I watched my diet and got plenty of exercise, I would be fine. He warned me, "Don't become a cardiac neurotic." I followed his directions and gradually began to feel well enough to resume my normal activities.

ERWIN'S ILLNESS

Erwin had always been healthy. He was slim and athletic-looking and could eat whatever he desired without gaining weight. One day he decided to donate his blood to the Red Cross. His blood was not accepted and he was sent to a hospital to have a biopsy of his bone marrow. To our horror, we found out that he suffered from a rare blood disease called Myelofibrosis. At that time the disease was not curable, although nowadays a bone marrow transplant can prevent it from running its deadly course. Erwin did some research and discovered that the average life expectancy for someone stricken with the disease was three years. He realized that he had undoubtedly contracted the disease as a consequence of being exposed to dangerous levels of radiation when Armour Research sent him to the Mojave Desert in California to examine and evaluate Notsnik, the USA's answer to Sputnik. In those days few were aware of the dangers that could be caused by radiation.

Our tranquil life had come to an end. Erwin soon had to stop working, and we had to give up our cultural and social activities one by one. He was in and out of the hospital, and a number of mistakes were made. He was given large doses of cortisone which added to his depression. I supported him as well as I could, conferring with his doctors, consulting with specialists, visiting regularly when he was in the hospital, and trying to keep up his spirits. In order to do this, I had to give up most of my professional activities, though I continued my private practice.

When Erwin was well enough to travel, we would fly to Key Biscayne, Florida, his favorite spot. We always stayed in the same hotel, a luxurious and comfortable place located near President Nixon's compound known as the Winter White House. When Nixon was there, the FBI took over the two top floors of our hotel to keep an eye on him, much to the chagrin of the vacationers who had to move out of their rooms. The warm air, sunshine, and relaxed atmosphere had a calming effect on Erwin. Although he was not healthy enough take part in the activities the peninsula had to offer, he hated to go home. Unfortunately we could never stay for more than two weeks at a time because I had to return to my private practice and he had to return to his physicians. As his illness progressed, we were no longer able to travel.

Somehow I managed to take care of the house, pay the bills, and keep my private practice going, but the joy had gone out of our lives. A number of our friends were very supportive, which helped us both. My analysis also helped me to have enough inner strength to sustain myself and continue to function.

Erwin fought hard for six years and never gave up. Towards the end he was in the hospital in a coma. I had asked the nurses to call me if there was any change and was at home catching up on my sleep. I awoke with a start at 4:00 AM and found out later that it was the exact moment when Erwin passed away. In one way, his death was a relief. Erwin was at peace, and I no longer had to watch him slowly deteriorate with no hope of recovery. Nevertheless, his death was a great blow to me. We had been very close and my need to go through the mourning period was paramount. At the same time I had to rework my past losses, of which there were quite a few. I made an appointment with my former analyst. After one session, he concluded that I did not need further analysis but could work on my losses by myself. His evaluation spoke to my inner strength, and my mourning period was not an extended one. Part of it had been accomplished while Erwin was still alive.

In spite of this, I was still depressed and exhausted both physically and emotionally. I decided that what I needed was to go on an extended trip. I joined the Council of Foreign Relations and signed up for a trip they sponsored to the Middle East.

After taking in all the sights in Cairo, we boarded a Greek ship and traveled through the Suez Canal to a port in the Red Sea where we took a bus to Luxor. There we visited the Karnak Temple Complex and crossed the Nile to view various anthropological sites including Queen Hatshepsut's Palace and the grave of Tutankhamun. We proceeded by ship to Jordan, where we visited Petra, the ancient site which we could reach only by horseback. From there we traveled to Jerusalem and Tel Aviv, afterwards visiting several of the Greek Islands and ending our trip in Athens.

The cruise was extraordinarily well organized. The cuisine was excellent, and my fellow travelers were a group of cultured, unassuming, and intelligent people. The Juilliard String Quartet played concerts for us every night, and we enjoyed frequent lectures from an Eastern specialist who traveled along with us as did the owner of the ship, who was a friend of Aristotle Onassis.

The trip, completely different from the last few years of my life, was therapeutic for me. It helped to restore my energy, and I returned much calmer than when I left. Along with my private practice, I resumed my work as a consultant to various schools, agencies, and individual practitioners and began to hold positions once again in various professional organizations. I gave seminars at the Institute for Psychoanalysis at their professional development programs, as well as at the SSA at the University of Chicago. Most of my friends continued to be supportive, accompanying me to cultural and social events, but a few dropped me, I'm not sure why.

FAMILY

My father, as you may remember, had a younger brother, Otto, who ran away from home, settled in New York City, changed his name to Arthur, married, had three sons, and never attempted to get in touch with my father again. My father's sister Aida, who emigrated to Cleveland, stayed in touch with Otto and his family and undertook frequent trips to Europe to visit us. When Aida died, Otto's son Arnold and Arnold's middle son Michael helped with the funeral arrangements. Michael, while looking through some of Aida's papers, came across the death announcement of my half-sister Martha which had my name on it. Arnold and his youngest son Joel flew to Vienna to look for me. At the Jewish Cultural Society in Vienna they were told that I had fled the Nazi regime by traveling to London. While in Vienna, they visited the famous cemetery where Beethoven is buried and found the graves of my father and Martha in the Jewish section of the cemetery. Their graves had been desecrated.

After returning home, Arnold began advertising in British newspapers, mentioning my name and asking if anyone knew where I was. Many people answered his advertisement but I was not among them. This went on for eight years. From time to time his wife Ruth said "enough already" and pleaded with him to stop, but Arnold persisted.

One warm summer's day not long after I had returned from a beautiful trip to Rio de Janeiro with a friend, I received a telephone call from my old friend Renate in London. She told me that my first cousin, Arnold Stein of New York City, had been looking for me for eight years. On a trip to the dentist, Renate had picked up a newspaper in the waiting room and had seen Arnold's advertisement. She talked to Arnold on the telephone and was convinced that he was indeed my cousin. She gave me his phone number.

I was thrilled by this incredible find. I called Arnold and invited him and Ruth to come and visit me in Glencoe. We had a touching and emotional reunion. Arnold looked very much like my father—tall and sturdy with similar facial features. Arnold and Ruth showed me pictures of their three sons and their families. All three sons were tall and well built. David, the oldest, lived in New York City and owned a reconstituted paper factory which he ran together with his wife. Both were former Shakespearean actors, and the advertisements for their goods and services read like the promotion piece for a theater performance. The middle son, Michael, had a master's degree in counseling and worked as the administrative director and fundraiser of a hospital conglomerate in Cooperstown, New York. His wife was a dealer in antique art books, a craft she learned from Mark Walberg, the host of *Antiques Roadshow* on PBS. The youngest son, Joel, worked for a radio station, played saxophone with a band, and later became a stockbroker. Arnold was in the insurance business and was about to retire from New York City to a large and comfortable house in Woodstock, New York.

After our initial meeting in Glencoe, we met at least once a year and talked on the telephone every week. I loved visiting them at their house in Woodstock, where all three brothers, their wives, and their children would convene for the occasion. It was a blessing and a privilege to be part of a family again, something I had been missing for many years, especially after Erwin's death. Their cultural taste was like my own, and I felt loved and accepted. What a pleasure to watch the grandchildren play happily in the backyard and in the pool while their fathers played instruments and sang songs that they themselves had composed. Woodstock, the town made famous by the hippies who gathered there in the 1960s, is a charming little town, inhabited by many retired artists and actors. The streets are lined with antique stores, art stores, and expensive boutiques. Flowers bloom everywhere, and a lot of people stopped by to visit with Arnold and Ruth on their way into town.

Arnold and Ruth drove me to many interesting historical landmarks in New York, including President Roosevelt's and Eleanor Roosevelt's homes in Hyde Park. When they traveled to Glencoe, I showed them the local sights including the Botanic Gardens, the Bahai Temple, and Ravinia, the summer home of the Chicago Symphony. One winter while Arnold and Ruth were sojourning in Florida, Ruth suffered a stroke which left her paralyzed and unable to speak. Arnold had to charter a plane to take her back home. Arnold, with the help of a nurse, took excellent care of Ruth at home, refusing to have her taken to a nursing home. One night, after laughing and dancing at his grandson's bar mitzvah, Arnold died of a heart attack. This came as a great shock to all of us. Like my father, he had seemed so strong and sturdy, and there were no signs that there was anything wrong with his heart. After some deliberation, David, Michael, and Joel reluctantly decided that Ruth would have to go into a nursing home, since they were unable to take care of her as their father had. Once in the nursing home, Ruth became more depressed, did not eat properly, and after a few months, died in her sleep. I am still in touch with all three brothers and their families, especially Michael who comes with his wife and daughter to visit from time to time.

Chapter Eleven

The Center for Psychoanalytic Study

In 1985 several mental health professionals, myself among them, were invited to be consultants to the Center for Psychoanalytic Study in Chicago, a relatively new institution whose founder had just resigned to return to his busy private practice.

The Center for Psychoanalytic Study was founded in 1981 by Peter Giovacchini, MD, along with his colleague, Alfred Flarsheim, a PhD psychologist. Dr. Giovacchini, a graduate of the Institute for Psychoanalysis, was a highly respected and widely known psychoanalyst. The author of thirty books and countless articles translated into German, French, Spanish, and Portuguese, he felt that a new and different institution was needed in Chicago. The Institute for Psychoanalysis did not treat severely disturbed patients and it only allowed MDs to become psychoanalysts. Dr. Giovacchini had proven through his own clinical work that psychoanalysis could greatly benefit the severely disturbed, and he, like Freud and practitioners in Europe and South America, believed that the rigorous training for psychoanalysis should be open not just to MDs but to social workers, psychologists, and other mental health professionals as well.

The Center for Psychoanalytic Study was located at McClurg Court, a newly built high-rise with spectacular views of Lake Michigan. Our group of consultants met there for several sessions to learn about the Center's aims, educational programs, and administrative practices. We were introduced to the newly appointed Executive Director James McGinnis, LCSW, and to various faculty members. I was excited by and impressed with the Center, with its faculty and their analytic way of thinking, with its focus on helping the severely disturbed, and with the fact that it encouraged other mental health professionals, not just MDs, to be trained as psychoanalysts. In addition to all of this, the Center was the first institution in the Middle West

137

authorized to grant a doctorate in psychoanalysis. Convinced that the faculty and administrators were open to new ideas, I wrote a detailed letter to Dr. Charles Shaiova, the Dean of Education, explaining my views on how to make the administration more efficient and how to improve and expand the curriculum. To my delight, he wrote me a very courteous letter asking me to join the Center and start teaching there.

MULTI-FOCUSING

I soon became thoroughly enmeshed in the Center and its many activities, taking classes, teaching classes, giving papers, attending the Professional Development programs, and continuing to think of ways to improve the Center, which I discussed with Jim McGinnis. Jim adopted quite a few of my suggestions and in 1989 appointed me to be his Associate Director, a position that included fundraising, recruiting more people for the board, and coping with the mounds of paperwork needed to satisfy the demands of the Illinois Board of Higher Education.

Whatever activity I was involved in, I found the atmosphere at the Center to be very stimulating. The candidates were highly motivated, well educated, and seasoned professionals—social workers, psychologists, and psychiatrists, some in private practice, some employed by social agencies. Most came from Illinois but some came from Michigan and Indiana and one flew in all the way from Atlanta to attend courses at the Center. Classes, which were small and intimate, were held on Fridays in order to accommodate the work schedules of both candidates and faculty.

The faculty was comprised of a distinguished group of psychoanalysts, social workers, psychologists, and psychiatrists, mostly from Chicago and its suburbs, who contributed their time pro bono, each teaching classes in his or her field of expertise. The only time a faculty member received a moderate remuneration was when conducting the analysis of a candidate or supervising a candidate's analysis of a control case. The esprit-de-corps among both candidates and faculty was high. All of us felt that one can never know too much about the human emotions, and we considered it a privilege to be part of an institution so highly regarded in the psychoanalytic community. Most of us participated in the Professional Development Program at the Center, and there was a constant cross-fertilization of knowledge and ideas. We did not emphasize any one psychoanalyst's concepts over the others. Instead, after making sure that our candidates were thoroughly grounded in Freud, we taught the conceptual framework of Object Relations which included Klein, Winnicott, Balint, Kernberg, Modell, and others. In addition to these, we taught Ego Psychology, Self Psychology as developed by Kohut, the concepts of Lacan, and most of the newly developed psychoanalytic methodologies. We allowed candidates to choose the one or ones that suited them best. This made for lively in-depth discussions and broadened the knowledge of candidates and faculty alike.

The Center granted a Certificate in Psychoanalysis as well as a Doctorate of Psychoanalysis (D.Psa.). In order to earn a certificate from the Center, each candidate had to undergo a personal analysis, take a prescribed sequence of courses under the guidance of an advisor, write some papers on an approved psychoanalytic concept, and treat at least two patients for a year and a half, later extended to two years, under the supervision of a training and supervising psychoanalyst. The fee paid by these "control cases" was minimal and so were the supervisors' fees. Most of the candidates working toward their certificate already had one or more graduate degrees. One outstanding candidate was a Catholic priest from Ireland who already had a doctorate in psychology. Another was Dr. Philip Giovacchini, Dr. Peter Giovacchini's son, who later joined our faculty.

As soon as I joined the Center, I began working toward my certification in psychoanalysis. I had completed my personal analysis but I still had to take more courses, write some papers, and treat two control cases, under the supervision of Dr. Peter Giovacchini, who had returned to the Center in the capacity of teacher and training and supervising analyst. I finished all the requirements for my certificate about the same time I was appointed Associate Director, but I spent several weeks waiting in frustrated suspense before Dr. Shaiova approved my major paper. In my capacity as Associate Director, I planned a tea-and-cake celebration at the Center for the graduates (including myself), their friends, and their families. It was a pleasant occasion, with a group of compatible people with similar interests and aims.

In 1992 Jim McGinnis decided to retire and move to the East Coast with his family. His wife, a trained analyst and graduate of the Center, wanted to be near her original family. This was a great loss for me, since Jim and I had an excellent working relationship. With the approval of the faculty and the board, I appointed Dr. Jerome Kavka, an analyst from the Institute for Psychoanalysis, to take Jim's place as Executive Director. Previously I had not been privy to the details of the financial situation at the Center. Now I had occasion to compare our income with our expenses and could see that the situation was precarious. This became critical when our rent at McClurg Court, already high, was raised to an amount we could not afford. Most board members and faculty members, seeing no way out, thought the time had come to close the Center down. I strongly felt that such a vital institution should not be allowed to die and tried to think what could be done to keep it going. As a first step, I volunteered to look for a less expensive location.

With the help of a real estate agent, I visited a number of impressive-looking, turn-of-the-century Chicago skyscrapers containing offices unsuitable for our purpose. Many provided toilets for men only. I wondered how the cleaning women and secretaries managed. One of the high-rises we looked at, famous for wholesale jewelry, had railroad tracks on most floors, where commodities were packed onto small trains, of no use whatever to those of us at the Center.

NEW QUARTERS

At last we found the ideal space, heartily approved of by our faculty and board—a three-room suite at the Spertus Institute of Jewish Studies at 610 South Michigan Avenue, near Roosevelt University and Columbia College and right across the street from Grant Park. Our main classroom was a large room with burlap-covered walls perfect for hanging pictures. Another large room did double duty as library and lecture room, and a small room became our therapy room used by candidates who did not have the facilities to treat their control cases. We furnished the rooms with donations from the faculty. Among these were an Eames easy chair, a Herman Miller couch, various art objects, a Japanese Shoji screen which we used to hide our storage area and filing cabinets, and six prints by Egon Schiele, which graced the burlap walls in the classroom. The overall effect was elegant yet comfortable. Best of all, our rent was considerably less than we had been paying at McClurg Court and our new landlords offered us free janitorial service and the use of additional classrooms and lecture halls. This facility gave the Center a new lease on life.

Soon after we had settled into our new suite, we applied for admission to the International Psychoanalytic Association (IPS), a prestigious organization in our field. They were favorably impressed. They admitted us on a provisional basis; however, the executive committee suggested that we add a few more courses to the curriculum and invite more analysts from the community to participate in our programs. Both of these suggestions worked out well, serving as checks and balances and providing us with a constant source of new ideas.

About this time Dr. Jerome Kavka introduced me to Irving B. Harris, a Chicago philanthropist with a gift for translating his vision into practical programs designed to improve people's lives. Harris had a special interest in child welfare and public policy and was instrumental in starting Project Head Start and the Harris School of Public Policy at the University of Chicago. I explained to Harris that our work at the Center included a special two-year program on Early Child Development, required of all candidates. I further explained that we, unlike most psychoanalytic institutes, did not separate the child analysts from the adult analysts, believing that adult analysts needed to understand early childhood development in order to have a more dynamic understanding of the adults they treated, and child analysts should be well grounded in adult analysis, since they frequently needed to treat the parents or caretakers of their patients. To our relief, Irving Harris agreed to support the Center with a generous yearly endowment. We also managed to obtain an endowment from Seymour Persky, the real estate mogul.

FUNDRAISING

To supplement these endowments, we continued our fundraising activities. Some of these centered on the arts. These included several events held at the home of Granvil and Marcia Specks, who have the largest collection of Expressionist prints in the country. Another event was held at the Block Gallery of Northwestern University when the first Gustav Klimt exhibit arrived, and I hosted several events at my house, focusing on my collection of Oriental art. At these events we always had a lecturer who emphasized psychoanalytic aspects of the art. On other occasions we attended avant-garde plays, blocking out a number of seats for our benefactors. Our board members and faculty attended most of these ventures and brought their family and friends.

Another fund-raising activity involved inviting well-known psychoanalysts to give lectures. There was Arnold Tobin, MD, from the Institute for Psychoanalysis, who spoke on the Post Traumatic Stress Syndrome and his experience with this symptomatology in the army. James S. Grotstein, MD, from California was scheduled to lecture on his concept of Black Holes, the state of mind of the severely depressed, but at the last moment he couldn't come and I was asked to read his paper for him. Other distinguished lecturers included our own faculty member, Richard D. Chessick, MD, PhD, of Northwestern University, who spoke on the famous analysis of James Joyce's daughter, and Bertram Karon, a PhD psychoanalyst and a dear supporter of the Center, who came from the University of Michigan on several occasions to speak on the treatment of severely disturbed patients. Dr. Giovacchini presented several papers on his work with schizophrenics, and I presented several papers on such topics as Melanie Klein, the Borderline Syndrome, and Transference and Counter Transference Issues. These lectures were given at the Art Institute, in hospitals, in various libraries on the North Shore, and in our own library at the Spertus Institute.

Yet another fundraiser was the innovative and stimulating professional seminars we held on a variety of current psychoanalytic subjects. These seminars, held at the Spertus Institute and the School of Social Work at Loyola University, were taught by our own faculty and were well attended by mental health professionals in the area. For all of our professional programs we offered CEU credits, which health professionals need in order to renew their license.

EXECUTIVE DIRECTOR

Dr. Kavka found the administrative responsibilities to be burdensome and turned over many of his duties to me. When he decided to leave in 1993, the board and faculty asked me to take his place.

In my new position, I continued to do activities I had already been doing for the Center such as dealing with paperwork, planning programs and curriculum, attending board meetings, organizing fund raisers, and presiding over faculty meetings. At the same time I was working on my doctorate degree. I had already met most of the requirements, having undergone a personal psychoanalysis and having taken two courses in statistics at the University of Chicago. I still had to finish the analysis of one of my control cases under the supervision of Dr. Peter Giovacchini, and I had to finish a clinical dissertation in which I proved my thesis by using a clinical example. This was a demanding task that took me three years to complete. My topic was "Losses in Infancy and Early Childhood Have a Lasting Effect on Child Development and Later Losses in Life." This I had to defend before my dissertation committee which consisted of Dr. Peter Giovacchini, Dr. Charles Turk, Dr. Jerome Kavka, Dr. Ner Littner, and Dr. Morris Sklansky. When I was awarded the Doctorate of Psychoanalysis (D.Psa.) in 1995, I planned a party at the Center, as I always did whenever anyone received a degree. On this happy occasion, there were three of us who received our doctorates at the same time.

Looking over the list of the Center's graduates, I see that we awarded twenty-three certificates in psychoanalysis and eight doctorates. Included among the graduates were social workers, psychologists, psychiatrists, and two psychiatric nurses with MAs, one of whom worked at a VA hospital with veterans suffering from Post Traumatic Stress Syndrome. She wrote her doctoral theses on this subject and was an outstanding clinician. Most of our candidates moved away from Chicago for a variety of reasons, but I am still in touch with quite a few of them. Their professional success is gratifying to me.

During the 1990s the Center was thriving. Our Professional Development Program was so well attended that we had to meet at libraries, hospitals, and universities to find auditoriums large enough to accommodate the crowd. Thanks to the Center's excellent reputation, outside speakers as well as faculty members were usually glad to work pro bono. We were highly esteemed not only by the psychoanalytic community but by the general mental health community as well. In the fall of 2000, when the Sigmund Freud exhibit was due to arrive in Chicago, the Field Museum of Natural History asked me, as a representative of the Center, to join an advisory panel. My advice was to make sure they had a woman psychoanalyst among their speakers. When the exhibit had been on display in Washington D.C., Gloria Steinem had publicly denigrated the exhibit, claiming—wrongly—that Freud was a male chauvinist. Having a woman analyst speak in Chicago served to counteract the damage Steinem had done.

QUICK SOLUTIONS

As time passed, our student body began to shrink, reflecting the fact that insurance companies refused to reimburse their clients for psychoanalytic treatment, which requires a minimum of three sessions a week. In reality, intense psychotherapy for a severely disturbed patient is a cost-effective procedure, since it frequently enables the patient to avoid being hospitalized. Nor is hospitalization always a good solution. Too often a patient, having received perfunctory treatment in the hospital, is dismissed prematurely, only to have to return again and again.

Although some patients were analyzed at reduced fees as the control cases at psychoanalytic institutes or by private practitioners who served a certain percentage of their patients at low fees, relatively few could be analyzed at these special rates. People wanted quick and inexpensive results, and there were new therapies such as Behavior Modification that claimed this as a "cure." The pharmaceutical companies also obliged, promising a wide range of miracle-producing pills.

In my experience, the therapies that claim quick cures only scratch the surface. Like medication, they treat the symptoms but do not help the therapist discover the underlying causes. Nor are drugs alone a good solution. There is scientific evidence that a patient who receives drugs with no accompanying psychotherapy is much worse off emotionally than one who receives psychotherapy as well. There are also countless examples of patients who, not wanting to be controlled by a pill, suddenly stop taking their medication, with disastrous results. I have seen many over-medicated patients whose symptoms are inhibited, along with their fantasies, delusions, and hallucinations. Consequently their therapist has little to work on and cannot even make an accurate diagnosis. Psychodynamic treatment, if expertly administered, decreases pathology rather than disguises it. My concern is that for patients a pill consciously or unconsciously represents an outside healer, someone other than themselves, whereas in analysis patients are taught how to work on their own problems, a process which is always difficult and often painful but which has lasting positive results. Although some emotional disturbances do make medication essential, there is no such thing as the ideal pill with an exclusively curative effect. In our current society, children especially are overmedicated, with detrimental results.

During the early eighties a young woman in her twenties, the daughter of a prominent family on the North Shore of Chicago, was referred to me. Edith had been hospitalized in the mental ward ten times and sent home with a medication called thorazine, only to return again and again. Every time she was readmitted to the hospital her thorazine dosage was increased. By the time I saw Edith, she looked and behaved like a zombie, shuffling her feet as she walked. This was called the "thorazine shuffle." Only after her doses of thorazine were slowly reduced and finally eliminated was she able to hear me and respond appropriately to psychotherapy. Edith eventually made progress. She was able to stay out of the hospital, hold down a job, make and keep friends, and lead a somewhat normal life. She continued to visit me after her parents pulled her out of therapy. Fortunately thorazine is no longer in use, but there are other medications which have similar effects.

CLOSING DOWN

In the fall of 2004 Irving Harris, our chief benefactor, died, and with his passing, the Center lost the yearly endowment he had so generously provided. Needless to say, we forged ahead, but I was getting older and my energy level had declined. The time had come for me to take stock of my life—to think about retiring from the Center and finding someone to take my place.

Looking around for a replacement was a disheartening undertaking. The members of the staff were all devoted to their tasks at hand but no one was interested in becoming the Executive Director. Although the Center continued to be a highly respected, scholarly, and clinically dynamic institution, some key faculty members who might have been willing to take on administrative duties had died recently, including Dr. Charles Shaiova and Dr. Peter Giovacchini. One reason that no one wanted the position was that there was no remuneration involved. Everyone at the Center worked pro bono, including me. As a matter of fact, when we were in the red, which we were from time to time, I was the one who turned the red into black.

I finally decided to ask the Institute for Psychoanalysis to take over our programs, especially the doctoral program, which the Institute badly wanted but had never managed to obtain. Armed with all the information about the Center, I made an appointment with the newly elected Director. Dr. X looked at all my papers and told me he would take my offer into consideration. Weeks passed but I never heard from him again. Everyone on his staff wanted to be able to grant the doctorate degree in psychoanalysis, but it never happened. Perhaps Dr. X felt overwhelmed by his new position and my offer was too much for him to cope with at that time. [1]

The closing of the Center was an exhausting, long-drawn-out, and depressing affair, and I had to accomplish it without much help from the faculty members, who were in a state of denial, unable to face the Center's inevitable end. With a heavy heart, I began to sell or donate to various institutions our furniture, our works of art, and all the books and journals in our large and comprehensive professional library. We used the money we made to pay our outstanding bills. Everyone at the Spertus Institute was sorry to see us move out and proclaimed that we were the best tenant they had ever had. We could not have asked for a better landlord. They were always most cooperative and supportive of all our wishes and demands.

I was sorry that this important chapter in my life was at an end, but I was glad that we had managed to continue for more than ten years after the rent was raised at McClurg Court. We had graduated a goodly number of candidates who went to cities all over the United States, acting as ambassadors of the Center's teachings and clinical approach. On a personal level, I felt blessed to have been able to contribute to and earn two graduate degrees in such a rich and stimulating environment. In my private practice I try never to turn a patient away and have had a number of severely disturbed patients referred to me by other analysts. Especially in these situations, I am able to make good use of all the knowledge I have acquired over the years in my profession.

In 1993, not long after we had moved into our suite at the Spertus Institute, the Center presented me with a plaque which reads as follows:

> Special Recognition Award Presented to Gertrude Pollitt, M.A. in appreciation and gratitude for your contributions toward the advancement of the field of psychoanalysis and The Center for Psychoanalytic Study

The plaque graces the wall of my office, where I see it every day.

NOTE

1. The Institute for Psychoanalysis did eventually open its doors to social workers, psychologists, and other mental health professionals to be trained in psychoanalysis, and other psychoanalytic training centers all over the USA followed suit. This change was in part brought about by the sparse attendance of MDs, who found the practice of medicine far more lucrative than the practice of psychoanalysis. General medical practitioners can see a patient for fifteen or twenty minutes and be reimbursed by insurance companies whereas an analytic session takes fifty minutes. Many insurance companies, in order to cut costs, were only willing to reimburse mental health professionals on a once-a-week basis, fine for those "quick fix" professionals who treat only the symptoms but not good for those devoted to treating underlying causes, which requires on the average three to five years of treatment with sessions three to four times a week. The Institute for Psychoanalysis still does not have the authority to award a doctorate degree sanctioned by the Illinois Board of Higher Education. In spite of this, there are still

many mental health professionals, primarily clinical social workers, who are willing to undergo the extensive training required to become a psychoanalyst—taking classes, being analyzed, and analyzing a small number of patients under close supervision by a trained analyst. I take my hat off to them for their determination, devotion, and investment of time. The Institute for Psychoanalysis has changed in another important respect. Like the Center for Psychoanalytic Study, they moved into the twentieth century. They have expanded their traditional curriculum to include not only Freud and Kohut but Object Relations theory and several more current theoretic frameworks. The latest innovation at the Institute for Psychoanalysis is that a female social worker was voted in as Director.

Chapter Twelve

Highland Park

While I was engaged in closing the Center for Psychoanalytic Study, I put my house on the market. The time had come when I no longer had the energy to maintain the house and garden properly. Erwin and I had lived there happily, a reflection of our solid and devoted marriage, and I had lived there happily alone for many years. Needless to say, my attachment to the house and everything in it was great. My real estate agent, Jennifer Noon, was an experienced, knowledgeable, and efficient woman who is still a good friend to the present day.

The house, well maintained with a beautiful garden, was within easy walking distance of the train station, a public grade school, a Catholic grade school, and a pleasant shopping center, making it particularly desirable for a young family. Although the housing market was somewhat shaky at the time, a more than adequate bid was made in a relatively short time and I had no choice but to graciously accept it. Jennifer and I searched in vain for a suitable apartment in Glencoe, but we did find a pleasant three-bedroom, two-bathroom apartment in nearby Highland Park. There was a livingroom-diningroom combination and a kitchen with a breakfast area, and I could turn one bedroom into an office where I could conduct my private practice. Best of all, there was a south-facing balcony that ran the length of the four rooms and had space for many of my indoor and outdoor plants. The outdoor swimming pool was some compensation for the spacious yard I had to give up.

ESTATE SALE

This was a stressful time for me. Moving to the apartment at the same time as closing the Center reactivated my separation anxiety. To make matters worse, I had to get rid of many of my cherished possessions because there would not be room for them in the apartment. I told myself that they were things, not people, but they were things with personal history attached, things I cared about greatly. Jennifer gave me the name of a firm that managed estate sales and enjoyed a good reputation. What we did not know was that the owner had recently retired and sold his business.

When the new owner, let's call her Cynthia, visited me several times to look over my many possessions, I was favorably impressed. She was attractive, well-spoken, well-groomed, and courteous, and seemed to understand how difficult it was for me to decide what to keep and what to sell. Eventually we had a complete list of which paintings, books, magazines, files, photographs, art objects, pieces of jewelry, kitchen utensils, garden equipment, cleaning supplies, mementos, and furniture I wanted to take with me and which I was willing to sell or give away. Cynthia seemed pleased and explained quite reasonably that she needed to earn a certain amount of money from the sale in order to meet her expenses and make a small profit. She estimated that the sale should yield at least $16,000.

Cynthia had several women who worked for her come to the house and put price tags on the various objects. She then invited me, along with her helpers, to a luncheon at my house. The lunch was both elegant and delicious—crab, shrimp, and lobster salad served on my best blue and white china—a lovely event, I thought, designed to keep up the morale of the workers. I did not start to wonder about Cynthia until she presented me with a large bill for the luncheon. My suspicions aroused, I checked the prices she had put on the antiques. Most of them were dramatically under-priced. Evidently her knowledge of antiques was scanty.

Since the house was to be used as a showcase for my belongings, I had to vacate the premises before the sale. It was a hurried move. I took basic supplies and most of my furniture with me to the apartment but left many things behind, to be moved later. I naturally assumed that Cynthia would be guided by the list we had made with so much thought and care. At this point, Cynthia told me in no uncertain terms that I was to stay away during the sale, which was to last two days, though I had suggested three, since there were so many items to sell. Ignoring her prohibition, I arrived early on the first morning of the sale to find interested buyers lined up outside the house waiting their turn to get in. Inside there were crowds of people swarming around everywhere. Evidently word had spread that there were good bargains to be had at the Pollitts' residence.

Amongst the many things I had put up for sale were some items I used for play therapy with the children I treated. Over the years I had accumulated quite a number of little dolls and doll furniture, far too many to take with me to my new abode. These sold quickly, and I was pleased to see them now in the hands of happy and gratified children, most of whom I knew from the neighborhood. I was not pleased, however, to see a $200 price tag on my "davenport," a small antique writing desk made of burled oak, built in 1823, and worth about $3,000. Furniture historians think that Captain Davenport, the Englishman who commissioned the design, may have been a sea captain who used his desk on board ship. Davenport desks have a secret drawer, several small drawers on the side, and a special place in back for storing large maps or navigational charts. I cherished this desk, which I had bought in England, and had no intention of letting it go for a small fraction of what it was worth. Evidently Cynthia was in the habit of disregarding the wishes of her clients. I immediately telephoned my colleague Dr. Chuck Turk and his wife to come with their SUV and trolley to rescue the desk. I stayed in the house for the rest of the day, removing price tags from items I wanted to take with me and hiding them in a corner of the kitchen to make sure they would not be sold. Among these was a yellow Lucite waste basket and matching tissue container that kept traveling back and forth between the items on display and my hiding place in the kitchen. At the end of the day I had the waste basket and Cynthia had the tissue box.

In the final reckoning, I discovered that Cynthia had sold or given away a number of items from the "Don't sell" list. Without consulting me, she had donated several of my sterling silver serving dishes, along with a valuable, pigskin-covered *Complete Works of Shakespeare*, to a hospital which refused to return them. Although my profit from the sale was not enough to cover my moving expenses, I am certain that Cynthia compensated herself generously for her efforts.

As an experienced therapist, I consider myself a good judge of character and it hit me hard that I had allowed myself to be fooled by a con artist, and an incompetent one at that. I wrote to the Better Business Bureau and threatened Cynthia with a law suit. Seemingly chastened, she returned a number of things, including some jewelry and two Meissen porcelain figurines, one dating from the 17th and one from the 18th century. She also tried to give me some items that belonged to someone else. Probably by this time she no longer had any idea of what belonged to whom. The last I saw of Cynthia, she was standing in the doorway of my apartment shedding crocodile tears for my benefit, an action which failed to win my sympathy.

APARTMENT

Moving into the apartment presented a new set of problems. In spite of having sold or given away so many items, I had collected a lot of things over the years and still had more possessions than the apartment could easily accommodate. An architect who is a good friend of mine came to the rescue. He helped me arrange my furniture, bookcases, books, art objects, and paintings in a very pleasing manner, and soon the new apartment began to look like home.

In some ways this was the easiest of my many moves. It was so close to Glencoe that I could see my Glencoe friends regularly and patronize the same library, theater, and stores. The neighbors on my floor of the apartment valued their privacy and did not welcome me with a home-baked pie as the neighbors in Glencoe had. Although my new neighbors were not in the habit of giving parties for each other, I gave several teas which they seemed to enjoy. When I stopped giving the teas, they took note and asked me why. One reason was that they never reciprocated. The other reason was that at the last party one woman had smirkingly said in a voice for all to hear, "Gertrude has a boy friend who visits her every Saturday morning at ten." This announcement met with dead silence. I did not bother to explain what was none of their business—that the "boy friend" was a patient of mine whom I'd been treating for several years.

ACTIVITIES

Although my energy was somewhat limited, I still served as a consultant to schools, agencies, and individual practitioners and as an on-call psychotherapist at Catholic Charities. My Co-Chair and Program Chair responsibilities continued with the Chicago chapter of ISPS (International Society for the Psychological and Social Treatments of Psychoses), and I often gave lectures at libraries, colleges, senior centers, temples, and the Institute for Psychoanalysis, as well as to the psychiatrists at the Evanston, Glenview, and Highland Park hospitals. When the Center closed, I decided to carry on with one course—the Film Viewing and Discussion Group, led by Ed Kaufman, LCSW, BCD. Ed and I always choose a film that deals with particular psychoanalytic themes such as ethical problems or developmental problems in childhood, adolescence, or adulthood. After the showing, Ed summarizes the film and leads a discussion. The course is well attended by experienced mental health professionals who can earn Continuing Education credits which some of them need in order to renew their license.

Most important to me is my private practice. I continue to treat a few adults in my home and even take on a new patient now and then. It is necessary to have good diagnostic skills in order to allow severely disturbed patients to come into your own home. I encourage my patients to express themselves through drawing, painting, or poetry, since this can be very therapeutic. One of my patients has given me permission to reprint two of her poems. The first, "Child," reveals her feelings about her traumatic childhood:

> In my mind I can see
> a small child alone who bleeds

Tears fall like rain
No one knows or hears the pain
There's a heart inside
that longs to love but in fear hides
A heart softly cries
in the night waiting for daylight
When the sun begins to rise
and the child opens her eyes
To hope that the morning light
will chase away the fears of the night
But only pain lingers on
in the heart of the little one
Oh God can someone know
that the child needs a hand to hold
and a gentle heart to reach inside
touch the wounds and calm the fright
Copyright © 1991

When her first therapist terminated this young woman without an adequate preparation, she expressed her sense of betrayal in this prose poem, entitled "An Agonizing Goodbye":

I am beside myself in pain. Lost within the depths of intolerable human agony. Trapped by the silent intensity of the horror within. I try desperately to grasp onto a hope beyond my terror's capacity to destroy. I wonder why God did not possess the mercy to allow me to die in my accident. I am haunted, tortured by an intense, unspeakable sense of isolation. I grieve endlessly over an emptiness and loss left by needs that were never responded to. Yearnings from my childhood strive to be recognized, responded to. I despair deeply over a profound sense of separation. I am overwhelmed by feelings of abandonment and helplessness. I am shocked that such inner hell could be triggered by an impending goodbye. It reactivated and reaffirmed my sense of inner isolation. I am terrified. Feelings from long ago rise up and relentlessly torment me. I feel injured, deserted and bereaved as intensely and defenselessly as a child. My internal horror rips me apart. The innermost part of me struggles for relief and there is no comfort to take refuge in.

This prose poem and other diagnostic material show this patient's extreme sensitivity to loss. Any loss in adulthood reactivates feelings from her childhood and she views it as abandonment, which in this particular case, it truly was. These two poems confirm the basic thesis of my doctoral dissertation—that separation and loss in early childhood have a great effect on the developmental growth process and on losses in later life.

Few practitioners have the patience and perseverance needed to treat severely traumatized patients. Such patients have the ability to zero in on their therapist's vulnerabilities, making it necessary for the therapist to carefully evaluate his or her responses. The therapist needs to seek consultation to clarify feelings that may have been reactivated within and to make sure that he or she has not over-identified with the patient. I do not give up on my patients. I am gratified by any improvement, no matter how small, and I always have hopes, which patients can identify with, that they will ultimately be able to function within their community and make a life for themselves.

Freud wrote that mental health requires that a person be able to love and to work. Dr. Morris Sklansky, a psychoanalyst and good friend of mine, took Freud's pronouncement one step further. He expounded the theory that mental health is like a stool with three legs. One leg represents the ability to love and make relationships. Another leg represents the ability to work and be gainfully employed. The third leg represents faith in a religion or a philosophy. If one leg is wobbly, it is cause for concern. If two legs are wobbly, the problems are serious.

As I look back on my long career as a mental health professional, I see my role as the catalyst through which patients become enabled to heal themselves. Occasionally former patients call or visit many years after the termination of their therapy to let me know that they are doing well. I find this extremely gratifying. They are living proof that pathology can be overcome.

Epilogue

During my long and eventful life I have climbed high mountains and crossed deep valleys. The mountains were the many dangerous and adverse situations I tried to conquer, and the valleys were the low points, the difficult times I had to tolerate and endure. People often express surprise that I was able to forge ahead no matter how difficult the circumstances and never capitulate to depression or despair.

In great part this is because I was blessed to be born into a loving, supportive, and prosperous family in Vienna, the cultural center of Europe which was at that time democratically and progressively governed. I was raised in a protective environment, which Dr. D.W. Winnicott termed a "holding environment." My parents and my caretakers encouraged me to express my feelings, including the negative ones. This gave me an inner sense of security and reinforced a healthy narcissism. Parents, caretakers, and relatives all enabled me to deal with the losses I experienced in childhood, helping me to get through the mourning period. When my sister died, my parents tried to soothe my pain and sustain me. When my governess resigned without any warning, my parents were there to comfort me. When my father died suddenly and unexpectedly, my mother was temporarily unavailable, but my aunt and uncle stood by me and my uncle introduced me to his world. Living through all these losses, though acutely painful, made it easy for me to empathize with the feelings of others and caused me to realize that no matter how bad things are at the time, they will eventually get better.

I internalized my parents' standards, wishes, and Weltanschauung. I am stubborn, pragmatic, flexible, and tolerant like my father, and like my mother, I have good organizational and administrative skills. Like both parents, I have become a collector of paintings and *objets d'art*. Like both, I value education, literature, and all the arts. Like them, I believe in the Jewish concept of Tzedakah—that what you receive from the community you should give back in whatever ways you can. I feel close to my cousins in the USA because they have an emotional and cultural background very similar to that of my primary family.

My psychoanalyst enabled me to further come to terms with my losses and helped me deal with the guilt I felt for not having rescued my family. It was he who enabled me to have enough inner strength to continue on the path of my family's hopes for me, the path I had chosen for myself—to help children, adolescents, and adults become emotionally healthy, productive human beings. This is my motivation. This is my calling. This is the mission I have tried to accomplish throughout my life.

People sometimes ask me why I never had children. When Erwin and I were first married, I did not feel mature enough to be a mother. When I terminated my analysis, I felt mature enough, but by that time I was too old. I did not wish to repeat the pattern of my parents who gave birth to me when Mother was forty-five and Father was sixty. I sublimated my maternal instincts by working with deprived, emotionally abandoned, and psychologically disturbed children. When Erwin died, I was sorry we had no children, and now that I am in my nineties, I wish I had children to keep me company and help me cope with the problems that come with old age.

Since I have no children of my own and lost most of my family when I was young, I am especially appreciative of the family I do have: Ruth and Arnold's sons, daughters-in-law, and grandchildren. I am glad that they feel close to each other, communicate with one another frequently, and get together often in spite of living in three different cities. I enjoy Arnold's grandchildren almost as if they were my own. The parents are not pushy but take their children's accomplishments in stride, and their accomplishments are impressive, fitting right in with the family tradition. All three grandsons are musicians, revealing a healthy identification with their musical fathers. One of the granddaughters, after working in advertising, has returned to school to obtain a second master's degree in industrial psychology, and the other granddaughter is a clinical social worker in private practice.

There are two things that continue to tear me apart. One is not knowing the fate of Aunt Paula, though, to tell the truth, I'm afraid to find out and would rather not know. The other is the conflicting feelings I experience towards Vienna. The Vienna of my childhood and early adolescence benefited me greatly, providing me with a rich cultural and intellectual education and proof that a good government can serve its people well. Vienna after the Anschluss was just the opposite. Nazi sadists were in command. Jews, so prominent in business, government, the arts, and the professions, were suddenly regarded as offal to be humiliated, beaten, robbed, deported, and gassed, as most of my relatives were. Viennese waltzes, songs by Schubert, sonatas by Mozart and Beethoven, all very dear to me, arouse dual feelings within me as I try with limited success not to let the hideous memories impinge on the beautiful ones.

I have outlived most of my friends and relatives and feel their loss deeply, though they still go on living inside me. In spite of limited energy and gradually deteriorating health, I want to go on living and being productive for as long as I possibly can. I go on in great part for the sake of my family, I go on living for them. Hitler never broke my spirit and he never will.

Appendix

1919: Gertrude's birth
1924: Martha's death
1931: Gerturde enters the real-gymnasium.
1932: Father's death
1934: Gertrude transfers to business school.
March 14, 1938: Anschluss in Vienna
March 17, 1939: Germany invades Czechoslovakia.
March 17, 1939: Gertrude flees to England.
March 1939: Gertrude obtains a job as a lady's companion.
April 1939: Gertrude becomes Lady Norton's scullery maid.
September 3, 1939: Great Britain declares war on Germany.
September 1939: Lady Norton leaves for France, and Gertrude is employed as the only maid in a boarding house.
September 1940: The Blitz begins.
Fall 1940: Erwin Pollitt comes to London. Gertrude works as Sammy's nanny.
May 1941: The worst of the Blitz is over.
December 7, 1941: Pearl Harbor
December 11, 1941: Germany declares war on the United States, and Erwin is en route to the USA.
1942: Gertrude works first as a flower maker, then as a flower seller.
1943: She becomes a nursery school teacher.
1943-1945: Gertrude receives a scholarship from the Czech Ministry of Social Welfare and studies at the London School of Economics in the department of social services.

May 8, 1945: VE Day. Gertrude leaves London for Normandy and then Germany to begin her work with UNRRA and the displaced persons program.

Summer of 1945: Gertrude arrives at Camp Foehrenwald and serves as Principal Social Welfare Officer in charge of teenagers.

Summer of 1946: Gertrude is promoted to Director of Camp Aschau and gradually is assigned five other DP camps to supervise, four of which are children's centers.

1947: UNRRA is taken over by IRO and Gertrude is promoted to a rank equivalent to major in the US Army.

1948: Gertrude returns to London and is appointed Director of the Lambeth Children's Cottage, under the auspices of St. Thomas Hospital.

November 1949: Gertrude emigrates to the United States and settles in Chicago.

January 13, 1951: Gertrude marries Erwin Pollitt.

1954: Receives BA from Roosevelt University, Chicago, while working as medical technician at the Northwestern University Medical School in the Cardiac Clinic

1956: MA from the University of Chicago School of Social Service Administration

1962: Certificate, Psychoanalytic Child Care Course, Institute for Psychoanalysis, Chicago

1956-1963: Gertrude has a one-year residency at the Jewish Children's Bureau of Chicago after which she is appointed to be a psychiatric social worker there. During these years she learns the fate of her uncle and mother, undergoes psychoanalysis, joins several professional organizations, and begins working for the growth of the profession.

1963: Moves to Glencoe, IL, establishes her own private practice, and continues to work with various professional organizations.

1977: Erwin's death

1985: Gertrude is asked to consult with the Center for Psychoanalytic Study in Chicago and becomes involved in all of their programs as a student, a teacher, a supervisor, and an administrator.

1989: Gertrude becomes a Certified Psychoanalyst and is appointed Associate Director of the Center for Psychoanalytic Study.

1991: Gertrude receives a plaque of recognition from the Center for Psychoanalytic Study for her contributions to psychoanalysis and the Center.

1993: Gertrude is appointed Executive Director of the Center for Psychoanalytic Study.

1995: Gertrude is awarded her doctorate in psychoanalysis from the Center for Psychoanalytic Study and becomes a training and supervising analyst at the Center.

2005: Center for Psychoanalytic Study closes down.

2005: Gertrude moves from Glencoe, IL, to Highland Park, IL.

2005 to the present: Gertrude conducts a small private practice and serves as therapist on call for the Catholic Charities. She is co-organizer of a Film Viewing and Discussion group for mental health professionals. She frequently gives lectures and presents papers in areas of her expertise in psychoanalysis to mental health professionals in national and international conventions, as well as to the general public. She serves as consultant to agencies and schools and to psychologists, social workers, and psychiatrists in private practice.

PROFESSIONAL AFFILIATIONS, PAST AND PRESENT

Member of the American Psychoanalytic Association (APsaA)

Member of the International Forum of Psychoanalytic Education (IFPE)

Co-founder, Co-chair, and Program Chair of the Chicago Chapter of the International Society for Psychological and Social Approaches to Psychosis (ISPS)

Member and Lecturer for the Chicago Association for Psychoanalytic Psychology (CAPP)

Chair of the Psychiatric and Mental Health Council (NASW)

Member of the American Association of Psychoanalytic Licensed Clinical Social Workers (AAPLCSW)

Chair and Program Chair of the Illinois Society for Licensed Clinical Social Work (ISLCSW)

Chair of the Private Practice Committee for the National Association of Social Workers (NASW)

Chair of North Suburban Service Council

Member of the Panel of Hearings of the Adjudication Committee (NASW)

Chair of the Committee on Practice Standards and Inquiry of the Illinois Society for Clinical Social Work (SCSW)

PUBLICATIONS

"Treatment of Child and Family Towards Intra-familial Adjustment." Child Welfare League of America, Case Record Exhibit 1956, in library of the League, used for teaching casework at the School of Social Service Administration, University of Chicago.

Article on Research Project on NASW members' opinion of private practice, published in *NASW Newsletter,* 1966, and in *Handbook in Private Practice of Social Work*, edited by National Association of Social

Workers, March 1967. Published in *Social Work Research & Abstracts*, the journal of the NASW.

"Emotional Implications in Physically Handicapped Students." Article published in *School Social Work Journal,* Vol. VII, No. 2, 1983, by the Illinois Association of School Social Workers.

"School Phobia." Article published in *School Social Work Journal* by the Illinois Association of School Social Workers, Vol. VIII, No. 2, 1984.

Book Review on *Theaters of the Mind* by Joyce McDougall, M.D., published in *Readings, A Journal of Reviews and Commentary in Mental Health*, published by the American Orthopsychiatric Association, Inc., first edition, 1986.

"Coalition of Social Work Psychoanalysts, Newsletter." Author and Editor, First Edition, May 1, 1988, New York, NY, a nationwide publication.

"The Influence of Separation Trauma in Infancy and Early Childhood." Editor and co-author of the book *Separation Trauma in Childhood* with Ner Littner, M.D., and Holly Johnston, PhD, Center for Psychoanalytic Study, 1992.